A
REVIVAL
OF
HOPE
IN THE
GENUINE
CHRIST

We have also a more sure word of prophecy;
Where unto ye do well that ye take heed,
as unto a light that shineth in a dark place,
until the day dawn,
and the day star arise in your hearts.
2 Peter 1:19

A
REVIVAL
OF
HOPE
IN THE
GENUINE
CHRIST

Real Hope for America in Crisis

Gary R. Goetz

WestBow
P R E S S
A DIVISION OF THOMAS NELSON

WestBow Press books may be ordered through booksellers or by contacting:

WestBow Press
A Division of Thomas Nelson
1663 Liberty Drive
Bloomington, IN 47403
www.westbowpress.com
1 (866) 928-1240

ISBN: 978-1-4908-1250-2 (sc)
ISBN: 978-1-4908-2496-3 (e)
Library of Congress Control Number: 2013918599

Printed in the United States of America.

WestBow Press rev. date: 1/24/2014

To:
the late Pastor F. H. Giles
of Marshfield, Wisconsin
whose teaching instilled in me early on
an interest in the prophetical portions
of the Word of God

Contents

Foreword

Romans 15:4 states:

> For whatsoever things were written aforetime were written
> for our learning, that we through patience and comfort of
> the scriptures might have hope.

A *Revival of Hope in the Genuine Christ* seeks to provide that hope and attach it to God's Word and what it has to say regarding future events. It is only by living with eternity in view that hope can be sustained! Gary Goetz seeks to encourage the unbeliever to find hope in Christ and the believer to find hope in the culmination of all things!

Dr. John L. Monroe
Senior Pastor
Faith Baptist Church
Taylors, South Carolina

Preface

Why another book about prophecy when there are many fine books on this subject in Christian bookstores already? First of all, the theme of prophecy and the coming of the Lord are immensely spiritually practical. With this in mind, this book seeks to link the need for spiritual revival and future events together. Revivals in American history in times of crises had a great influence on American culture. The crisis in America today becomes greater as we move closer to the end of the age. According to the Word of God future events should do more than satisfy our curiosity. We should not be occupied in trying to identify the Antichrist, or 666, or be survivalists waiting for a world crisis. This would repeat the error of the early Thessalonian believers, who stopped their normal duties and therefore became unfaithful in the service of Christ. The apostle Peter, in the light of the future dissolution of this present order, stated:

> Seeing then that all these things shall be dissolved, what manner of persons ought ye to be in all holy conversation and godliness (2 Peter 3:11).[1]

The book of 1 Thessalonians mentions the coming of Christ in every chapter making eschatology, or future events, the theme of this book. There are exhortations to be faithful to the Lord along with encouraging spiritual living through continual rejoicing, prayer, and thanksgiving indicating eschatology has practical applications.

> Rejoice evermore. Pray without ceasing. In everything give thanks: for this is the will of God in Christ Jesus concerning you (1 Thessalonians 5:16-18).

The coming of Christ is the future hope that should keep us aware that this world is not our home and that we should never become focused on worldly endeavors. We should be focused on the edification of other believers and the proclamation of the Good News of the gospel of Christ. This book emphasizes that hope for America is an individual hope in the gospel of Christ and His coming kingdom. It also focuses on the need for a revival involving growth of faith in Christ and Spirit-filled living among believers to prepare us for the next great prophetic event—the Rapture.

Secondly, this has been written to attempt to enhance our understanding of our future life in the kingdom of Christ. The Bible presents the program of God as a series of ages, or periods of time.[2] We now live in the church age and are moving to the second coming of Christ followed by the millennial age on this present existing earth. Old Testament believers and those of the church age will rule with Christ from the New Jerusalem. Heaven is a city called the New Jerusalem where believers in their new bodies will dwell and intermingle with people in their natural bodies during the Millennium.

Three things are true of the future age with Christ:

1. It will be "face to face" knowledge of Christ that supersedes the knowledge that we have of God through the present written revelation of Him.

For now we see through a glass, darkly; but then face
to face: now I know in part; but then shall I know
even as also I am known (1 Corinthians 13:12).

2. Both believers and unbelievers will be rewarded
    according to their works. Salvation is by faith alone
    apart from works. However, the believer will still
    appear at the Judgment Seat of Christ in heaven
    for rewards while the unbeliever will be subject to
    degrees of judgment in hell for eternity.

    For the Son of man shall come in the glory of his
    Father with his angels; and then he shall reward every
    man according to his works (Matthew 16:27).

3. In the ages to come through the eternal state, the
    purpose of God is to demonstrate the multifaceted
    aspects of the riches of His grace in Christ.

    That in the ages to come he might shew the exceeding
    riches of his grace in his kindness toward us through
    Christ Jesus (Ephesians 2:7).

Therefore, we need to start today to praise Him for His
marvelous grace. Praise will be the great occupation of those
who inhabit the heavenly city, the New Jerusalem. Praise of
God will supersede any work accomplished for God in the
millennial age.

From The Tribulation To The Millennium*

X Signing of the Covenant w/Anti-Christ by Jews starts the…	Anti-Christ breaks Covenant starts the 2nd half called the Great Tribulation	2nd Coming of Christ with the Church ends the 7 yr. Tribulation and starts the 75 Days	Judgments following 2nd Coming during the…	1000 year Millennial Reign of Christ
7 year Tribulation Period			…75 Days	
3 ½ yrs = 1260 days**	2nd half = 1260 days*		Rev. 19:11-16 Dan. 12:11-12	
Daniel 70th Week*** Dan. 9:27 Matt. 24:15-21; 2 Thess. 2:4				

*Chart created by author

**From the Jewish calendar: a month is always 30 days ***A Jewish week of 7 Years

Ages to Come--Prophetic Timeline*

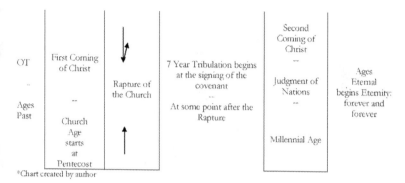

OT

..

Ages
Past

First Coming
of Christ

..

Church
Age
starts
at
Pentecost

Rapture of
the Church

7 Year Tribulation begins
at the signing of the
covenant

...

At some point after the
Rapture

Second
Coming of
Christ

--

Judgment of
Nations

--

Millennial Age

Ages
Eternal
begins Eternity:
forever and
forever

*Chart created by author

- Old Testament—ages past
- Christ's first coming led to the present church age at the day of Pentecost[3]
- Pre-tribulation Rapture takes place at God's choosing[4]
- 7-year Tribulation starts at some point after the Rapture with the signing of the covenant[5]
- Second coming of Christ followed by the judgment of the nations and the millennial age (1,000 year reign after the 7 years of tribulation)
- The Eternal kingdom after the Millennium, believers live forever with Christ

The Panorama of the Ages*

Age / Dispensation		Judgment	
Innocence	Gen. 1:28	Fall of Man	Gen. 3:6-7
Conscience	Gen. 3:7	Flood	Gen. 7:17-18
Human Government	Gen. 8:15	Tower of Babel Scattering	Gen. 11:1-8
Promise	Gen. 12:1	Israel in Bondage to Egypt (Promise to be Fulfilled)	Ex. 1:8-11
		Israel Delivered from Egypt	Ex. 12:31-51
Law	Ex. 19-20	Jerusalem Under Gentile Control	Luke 21:24
Church Age (Promise Fulfilled to Gentiles)	Matt. 16:18	Leaven Permeates Producing a False Church	Matt. 13:33 Rev. 17
7 yr. Tribulation	Dan. 9:27	Intermediate Period Between the Church Age and the Millennium	Dan. 9:27
1,000 yr. New Millennial Age (Promise Fulfilled to Israel)	Rev. 20:6	Nations Rebel Under Satan Great White Throne	Rev. 19:11-20:15
		Judgment Destruction of Present Earth and Heavens	2 Pet 3:10
The Eternal State: New Jerusalem Descends	Rev. 21:2	God is "ALL in ALL" Last Enemy of Death Destroyed	I Cor. 15:24-28

*Chart created by author

Acknowledgements

First and foremost, I would like to thank my wife, Peggy, for her loving support in working with me on the production of both my doctoral dissertation and this book. I could not have accomplished it without her.

I also want to thank my pastor emeritus of Faith Baptist Church Dr. John Vaughn for his personal encouragement and help in various ways as well as my present pastor Dr. John Monroe for his expository teaching of the Word of God along with his encouragement to write. Included are all the fundamental and evangelical writers that I have studied throughout my life. Knowledge is always engaged as a building block and is intermingled with the research of others.

Thanks will forever go to my late parents Ray and Beatrice Goetz for the practical, godly example exemplified by their gift of hospitality to visiting missionaries and pastors in our home. They modeled Christ to their six children who all are serving the Lord in various capacities.

And then there is my life-long friend Jim Dodge who unselfishly helped in *planting a seed* for writing.

Most of all I would like to thank the Lord for His patience and grace working and bringing personal revivals in my own life when I began to stray from His will.

Introduction

The Good in America

America has traditionally been a land of hope and opportunity for all ethnic groups. From the very beginning of the settling our shores people came seeking both religious freedom and economic opportunity. This continues as immigrants from other lands come seeking "The American Dream." America remains superior in many ways. First of all, our country is the most humanitarian and compassionate nation in the world. Whenever tragic events occur either at home or abroad our country is on the firing line with disaster relief. Secondly, our country has used resources to fight for freedom and democracy around the world. Although transplanting democracy into other countries that have no past foundation for it may have questionable results, the fact remains that our leaders have had the vision of freedom for other countries. Most importantly, our country has continually stood with other viable democracies in the world such as Israel and the United Kingdom.

Real permanent hope for America and the world is an individual hope in the person of Jesus Christ. Thankfully, this good news of salvation in Jesus Christ is still preached in many churches across America today. The Bible teaches that there is a new age of peace and prosperity coming to the world through the arrival of Christ's kingdom on this present earth. Believers in Christ living in the church age will participate in this future age. The Bible promises that the church, defined as every believer in Christ and not a particular individual denomination, will live and rule with Christ from the New Jerusalem on this present earth for one thousand years as recorded in Revelation 20:6:

> Blessed and holy is he that hath part in the first resurrection: on such the second death hath no power, but they shall be priests of God and of Christ, and shall reign with him a thousand years.

Ruling with Christ awaits the believer in this future event. For now, believers are to be servants according to the example of Christ as seen in Mark 10:45:

> For even the Son of man came not to be ministered unto, but to minister, and to give his life a ransom for many.

The Real New Age is Coming

Before the coming of the genuine real new age of peace and prosperity on earth, a pseudo new age under the Antichrist will engulf the world. It will be an unparalleled age of deception in the history of man in which the vexing Israeli-Palestinian conflict will appear to be solved and world-wide unity will seem to be realized. Christ Himself warned of the deception to come in Matthew 24:23-24:

> Then if any man shall say unto you, Lo, here is Christ, or there; believe it not. For there shall arise false Christs, and false

prophets, and shall shew great signs and wonders; insomuch
that, if it were possible, they shall deceive the very elect.

This deception is made possible through rejection of the
truth about the salvation of God in Christ.

And with all deceivableness of unrighteousness in them
that perish; because they received not the love of the truth,
that they might be saved. And for this cause God will
send them strong delusion, that they should believe a lie
(2 Thessalonians 2:10-11).

The words *a lie* in the original Greek includes the article
making it *the lie*. This *lie* proposes that a mere man, other
than the genuine Christ, is God. This coming new age of
deception was alluded to by presidential republican candidate
Rick Santorum in his political campaign when he spoke of a
new theology overtaking America which is not based on the
Bible.[1] This new theology rejects the written revelation of
the Bible. This postmodern view is based on experience and
intuition. Furthermore, it is centered in a Western form of
Eastern mysticism and pantheism while teaching the doctrine
of monism which declares that the whole earth, including
man, *is* God. It contends that man is god-like and can alter
consciousness to access the god that is in all man-kind. This
new religious theology is concerned with saving the planet and
environment and comes by way of the United Nations, which
champions nuclear disarmament along with green energy. The
UN is more concerned about saving the planet than saving
the individual soul. It is beyond the scope of this book to
give a complete exposé on New Age religious theology as
others have written entire books.[2] The following is a concise
definition of New Age theology by author Elliott Miller:[3]

Starting with humanistic and evolutionary assumptions, it is global (rather than national) in its perspective, and is concerned above all with threats to world survival. Its distinctive emphasis is finding holistic solutions to planetary problems, and this concern usually culminates in the vision of a united world community.

Before the genuine new age arrives, the world will go through a valley of trouble called the Great Tribulation because they have rejected the genuine Christ and accepted the Antichrist who rides to power on this "new theology" of a "united world community."

The "New Theology" by Global Government

As the world moves to a new socialist state, people will increasingly look to global government for answers to the vexing economic and social problems in the world. Dick Morris, who often appeared as a commentator on Fox News, warns of global government and the threat of the loss of freedom to the US.[4]

Advancing in the name of environmentalism, social justice and sustainability, the Globalists and Socialists-who run the UN, are proceeding apace with their far reaching game plan to end national sovereignty and subsume all nations under global governance.

Author William Jasper has written extensively on subjects ranging from the European Community to the New World Order. He states:[5]

The true, imminent danger to America and to all nations seeking peace and good will stems from the widespread acceptance of the monstrous falsehood that in order to live in an 'interdependent' world, all nation-states must yield their sovereignty to the United Nations.

The US has been made subject to the international law of the UN. One of the first acts that President Obama performed, very early in his first term, was to sign agreements with the UN making the US subject to international law. Pamela Geller states:[6]

> In a world that generally values the freedom of speech, as well as the freedom of conscience and the legal equality of all people, far less than does the United States of America, the implications of this are clear: erasing the distinctions between American law and international law would mean an erosion of the rights and freedoms of Americans, and a concomitant deterioration of American society.

The Rule of the Genuine Messiah

However, the Bible predicts that a genuine new era of peace and prosperity is coming to the world through the rule of the Messiah Christ. The world is now on a quickening path to the coming of Christ and His kingdom. There is a destination and goal for mankind. The better part of wisdom and valor would encourage us to be in lockstep with the program of God, who has made known His program for the destiny of mankind through the Scriptures.

> Having made known unto us the mystery of his will, according to his good pleasure which he hath purposed in himself: That in the dispensation of the fullness of times he might gather together in one all things in Christ, both

which are in heaven, and which are on earth; even in him (Ephesians 1:9-10).

Revival of American Christianity in Times of Crises Past and Present

Moving from the prophetical to the historical, it cannot be denied historically that Christian revivals took place at crucial junctures of American history. The first identified Great Awakening took place before America was founded and helped prepare our country for the Revolution. The Second Great Awakening took place before the Civil War and thus helped prepare our country in crisis. The nationwide Businessmen's Prayer Revival, beginning in 1857, also preceded the Civil War and prepared our country for the two world wars along with preparing the Christian world for the arrival of religious liberalism in the Protestant church. The Bible Institute and Bible College Movements along with a great Christian mission outreach followed the Businessmen's Prayer Revival. Bible colleges were needed to combat religious liberalism which had pervaded Christian colleges and seminaries. While pluralism now permeates our American society, that very diversity is a result of religious freedom in America. However, it is the Judeo-Christian ethic that has made our country exceptional and is the basis for freedom and a genuine democracy in which man can govern himself.

Today it is apparent that America is in a moral and economic crisis. Some Christians are questioning whether we can have another nationwide revival of Christianity. This writing examines briefly revivals in the past to see whether we individually qualify for spiritual revival. Certainly there have been individual church revivals, and we can and should have spiritual revival in our own hearts. However, we will have to move past our tepid prayers and tepid love for our God, fellow man, and our comfort zone in this world. May the Lord start a *fire* in our own hearts and a *passion* for God along with a *desire* to serve our fellow man. Remember the lessons of history! Revivals of Christian faith start with individuals. Hope for America is primarily hope for the individual in a world where many have lost hope.

What In The World
Has Gone Wrong?

Is the American ideal and dream now fading and therefore becoming elusive for many? There is obvious uneasiness in the Republic today among the thinking populace about the direction America is taking. At the time of this writing, congress has passed a bill raising the debt ceiling 2.4 trillion while proposing immediate cuts for a lesser amount. The stock market almost immediately showed its lack of confidence in the bill by falling, and this was coupled with a low Gross National Product report. Although fiscal conservatism in government is a good thing, the ultimate solution to the problems in America does not lie primarily in the Tea Party or in a particular political candidate or in a particular political action but in a true spiritual revival in the hearts of men. America is now in a moral and spiritual malaise since moving away from the Christian principles that upon which our country was founded. America's greatness has not been due to a powerful military or GNP or the intelligence of leaders, although America does have a powerful military and many capable leaders. Greatness has been connected to the Christian heritage of America. This is a nation in which there are still many churches teaching the truth of the Good News of the death and resurrection of Jesus Christ. Churches have sent and are still sending out missionaries with this Good News.

As already noted, America is the most humanitarian nation in the world, and it would seem like this would not be overlooked by God. Our country supports God's biblically-chosen nation, Israel.[1] The fact that God chose Israel does not mean they are inherently better than the Gentiles. It is not a miracle that God saves or chooses some, it is a miracle that He saves or chooses any. In salvation, the mercy of God is controlled by His sovereign will.[2] Today the nation of Israel has been set aside by God as His vehicle of blessing to the world, but there is a future day when they will be restored to that privileged condition.[3] In this present church age all people who believe on Christ are on equal level, and there is no distinction or superiority of any nation or individual.[4] People who do not believe in Christ are still loved by God; His sovereign will does not preclude the prevenient grace of God given to all men who would choose to accept Christ as the Messiah.[5] If any nation is blessed by God they will need to be in harmony with the will of God on the earth for men. This will of God is that all men be saved and come to the knowledge of the truth about Himself.[6] Our primary responsibility to the leaders of our country is to pray for them because they are in the category of those whom God desires to be saved and come to the knowledge of the truth.

Crises for America from Without

Although there is genuine hope for individuals and for America as a nation, America certainly is in crisis today from without her borders. At the time of this writing, anti-Americanism is being demonstrated by protests in North

Africa and the Middle East. Terrorism continues to be a vexing problem. In addition to this, Iran seeks to obtain nuclear weapons and sponsors terrorism. Despite the fact that many view the Cold War as a thing of the past, tensions between the US and Russia seem to be on the increase. Russia arms terrorism supporters like Iran and Syria. And, both Russia and China refuse to support UN sanctions on Syria even though Syria is brutally slaughtering dissidents in their own country.[7]

In an interview with author Gordon G. Chang on Fox News, Mr. Chang contends that Russia and China support rogue states like Iran and North Korea and should be viewed with concern as major players in world events.[8]

Also, some believe that Israel will launch an attack on Iran's, nuclear sites even without the help of the US.[9] It would seem that the US will not be able to avoid being drawn into a conflict between Israel and Iran if this should happen.

The Need for a Spiritual Revival and Genuine Hope

In a pluralistic society, the very idea of absolute truth in a person may sound strange to some. However, the Bible champions hope based on truth for the believer both in the present and for the future. There must be an audacity to hope. Real permanent hope is not in political systems but in the God of truth of the Old and New Testaments. The Bible offers hope for the believer for both the present age and the future ages to come. There is a plethora of ancient Hebrew words in the Old Testament for faith connected with hope. These words have the idea of *trust* in God, to be "confident" and "safe" in God, to have *hope* by taking *refuge* in God, while having an eager expectation in God longingly waiting for

Him to act. All this is based upon the fact that, while God is great beyond comprehension, He is also characterized by loving kindness which is connected to His faithfulness to His Word. This is true because of the covenant which He had made with His own people. One Hebrew word for *hope* and *faith* means to "rely" or "lean on" or "to feel confident," "safe," and "secure."[10] This same Hebrew word is also used of the *false hopes* which bring a "false sense of security" to men which will ultimately result in disappointment and shame. Some false hopes which bring a false sense of security include hope in man, violence and oppression, riches, idols, military power, religion, one's own righteousness, and foreign alliances. Conversely the hope laid out for the believer will result in a joyous, future fulfillment.[11]

I Have Seen The Enemy—It Is "I"

The Crises in America from Within

The most insidious dangers are the threats from within which may not be as obvious as the threats without. The late radio commentator Paul Harvey spoke of how America could be seduced by the Prince of Darkness. This speech was broadcast by the legendary ABC Radio commentator on April 3, 1965: [1] The essence of the speech was that the devil's biggest goal is to take over the US. He would do this by promoting a self-seeking lifestyle while promoting the Bible as a myth to the young. Furthermore, he would blur distinctions between good and evil and teach the old to pray: our father which is in Washington. In addition to this, he would get the courts to rule against God, in favor of pornography, and evict God from government and the schools. In the churches he would substitute psychology for religion and in the world he would make science a god. Finally he would take from those who have and give to those who want until he had destroyed all incentive and put all in slave camps.

America under Judgment

According to the objective truth of the Bible, the sobering reality is that America is already under the judgment of God, and its prominence among nations may be short lived. This may be regarded to be a negative assessment, but when America is weighed in the balances of God's scales, according to objective truth, it cannot be denied that God must already be acting. Whenever truth is turned on its head and moral absolutes are denied, the downward slide is to skew ideas and philosophies about life. This is demonstrated by statements from the Old and New Testaments.

> And even as they did not like to retain God in their knowledge, God gave them over [the Greek word for *gave them over* means a *judicial act of judgment*] to a reprobate mind, to do those things which are not convenient (Romans 1:28).[2]

A reprobate mind is a mind which is disapproved by God which causes one not only to practice immorality, but also to argue for its legitimacy and for the fact that it needs to be accepted as just another alternative lifestyle. All this is argued for in the name of our "rights."

The Bible emphasizes our responsibilities over our rights. Although the past civil rights movement was used by God to overcome prejudice against minorities, the movement has taken a wild swing from an emphasis on responsibilities to an emphasis on rights. In reality, we do not have "rights" from God because; we are rebellious sinners who do not deserve His grace.

> It is of the LORD's mercies that we are not consumed, because his compassions fail not (Lamentations 3:22).

Although human rights are considered a fundamental to democracy and are demanded in the UN Charter, Christianity encourages man to give their "rights" to God and He will give them back as privileges.

Tolerance has replaced truth in our American society. Pluralism has become the watch word, but it is a type of agnostic pluralism that questions whether anyone can say there is one true God and only one way to God as Jesus claimed.[3] We are free to believe or not believe that Christ is the only way to God. Biblical Christianity recognizes the freedom of man to choose as Jesus said, "whosoever will, may come." If the word pluralism is used to mean there are many different religions and philosophic viewpoints in America today, as opposed to the religious Christian protestant influence, which so greatly influenced the framers of our Constitution at America's beginning, this definition is certainly true. However, that does make them all equally valid. The prophet Isaiah pronounces a *woe* upon those who turn the truth on its head proclaiming what God has said to be evil, to be good.

> Woe unto them that call evil good, and good evil; that put darkness for light, and light for darkness; that who put bitter for sweet, and sweet for bitter! (Isaiah 5:20).

Political correctness is simply the approval of the state upon the prevailing philosophy in society including moral relativism, or denial of moral absolutes. Sadly, this presently exists among the intellectually elite in many colleges and universities today. However, these morally relative views are not shared by many in the general populace. Political correctness has arrived because we now live in a postmodern world in which it is claimed that there is no objective truth. This philosophy proposes the idea that what may be truth for me may not be true for you.[4] Accompanying this philosophy has been the shift by the state in the promotion of the rights of gender and races of people to promoting the rights of alternative moral lifestyles.

Freedom of Religion is Freedom for Religion from State Control

The framers of our constitution saw the wisdom of disestablishing religion from state control. The Protestant Reformation in Europe still retained the tie of one religion to the state. Examples are the Anglican Church of England and the Lutheran Church of Germany. Denominational intolerance traveled to America as Baptists were persecuted in America at its beginning, partly because of their idea that baptism must follow belief as opposed to the infant baptism as practiced by the Anglicans, Congregationalists, and Presbyterians. The Separatists and Puritans who arrived on American shores in its early history came because of their desire to have freedom to worship according to their conscience. This was largely restricted in England by the established religious order that sought out those who desired to stand for the truth of God, for their belief they were persecuted and even martyred. Our founders wanted, as an end result, freedom *for* religion, not freedom *from* religion. Our founders did not want to eliminate God from the public square. They did, however, want to prevent one religious denomination from state sponsorship.

The Loss of Influence of Biblical Christianity in the Intellectual Arena

Biblical Christianity, although still believed by many on the grass roots level in America, has in practicality lost much of its influence on our country in the intellectual arena. A demonstration of this is exemplified by modern psychology. Psychology has filled the vacuum of a rejected biblical outlook and has ascended, in practical influence, over religion in society. This is true despite the fact that psychology acknowledges that it has no universal absolute measurement of abnormal behaviour. Ronald Cromer in *Abnormal Psychology* states: [5]

> Abnormal behaviour violates a society's idea about proper functioning. Each society establishes norms (explicit and implicit rules for appropriate conduct). The focus on social values as a yardstick for measuring deviance suggests that the judgments of abnormality vary from society to society.

Psychiatrist Keith Ablow objected to the use of the term *evil* to describe the mass school shooting at Newtown, Connecticut. He described it instead as *mental illness visiting the town* of Newtown. [6]

Although modern psychology has been a relatively late arrival in history (1879), it exerts a powerful influence over every academic discipline today ranging from the medical field to education and business. Psychologists are often interviewed on television to get their explanations of the cause of horrific crimes and world problems. Psychologists rather than ministers now seem to be the "experts" on human behavior and happiness. Pop television psychologists, such as Dr. Phil, give dogmatic prescriptions for happiness in marriage and other areas. [7] Although psychology is helpful in the medical and measurement area, the discipline itself has a philosophic element to it of which we would do well to be wary. Influential men in the early history of psychology such as William Wundt and William James were philosophers and educators. Major founders of modern psychological thought such as Sigmund

Freud, Carl Rogers, and Carl Jung were not believers in the Bible.[8]

The Replacement of Truth with a Lie

Life cannot be lived in a vacuum if the truth is rejected; therefore a lie will take its place and exert a practical influence over a life resulting in the worship and love of self rather than love for the true God.

> Who changed the truth of God into a lie, and worshipped and served the creature [creation] more than the Creator, who is blessed forever. Amen (Romans 1:25).

Love of oneself is the natural condition of man. The Bible assumes self-love; it does not command it. "For no man ever yet hated his own flesh; but nourisheth and cherishith it . . ." (Ephesians 5:29a). This natural tendency of love for self will be on the increase and flourish in the last days:

> This know also, that in the last days perilous times shall come. For men shall be lovers of their own selves . . . (2 Timothy 3:1-2a).

Today, the lie that is promoted by modern psychology is that our greatest need is self-love. However the truth is that we fail to love God and others as God commands. This is as fundamental as the Old Testament law and has been raised to a new level in the New Testament by Christ. Christ said the greatest commandment of the Law was to love God and to love others. Furthermore, love for fellow believers is to be fashioned after the love Christ has for His own.

Jesus said unto him, Thou shalt love the Lord thy God with all thy heart, and with all thy soul, and with all thy mind. This is the first and great commandment. And the second is like unto it, Thou shalt love thy neighbor as thyself (Matthew 22:37-39).

A new commandment I give unto you, That ye love one another; as I have loved you, that ye also love one another (John 13:34).

A Subtle Pressure on American Christianity

In conclusion, America is in a crisis in the religious and moral realm today. Although Americans are incurably religious, religion needs to be "transformed" into spiritual living practicality. The culture, with its careless hedonism and materialistic outlook involving love of self, has combined with agnostic pluralism and political correctness to put a subtle pressure on those who say they believe in the authority of the Bible. At the end of this present age the Bible says:

And because iniquity shall abound, the love of many shall wax cold (Matthew 24:12).

The Greek word for love is *agape* which means "God-like unselfish love." This verse implies that it is the love of the believer for God and Christ that will grow cold; consequently, the believer's love for others will grow cold, also.

History Does—
Repeat Itself

Ancient Bible History and Today

The end of this age is compared to the ancient days of Noah
and Lot and the judgments that followed.

> And as it was in the days of Noah, so shall it be also in
> the days of the Son of man. They did eat, they drank, they
> married wives, and they were given in marriage, until the
> day that Noah entered the ark, and the flood came, and
> destroyed them all. Likewise also as it was in the days of
> Lot; they did eat, they drank, they bought, they sold, they
> planted, they builded; But the same day that Lot went out
> of Sodom, it rained fire and brimstone from heaven, and
> destroyed them all. Even thus shall it be in the day when
> the Son of man is revealed (Luke 17:26-30).

The sobering fact is that these ancient judgments
occurred before there was any written revelation of God
such as contained in our modern day Bible. Yet, over two
millennia after Christ and a written revelation of Him, the
present age in the Western world has regressed, in practicality,

to the condition of the days of Noah and Lot. The basic manifestations of the days of Noah and Lot were a careless hedonism with violence and a lack of respect for human life. Regarding the days of Noah, Genesis 6:11 states:

> The earth also was corrupt before God, and the earth was filled with violence.

A Careless Hedonism

Hedonism comes from the Greek word for lusts (*hēdonē*) which is used in James 4:1:

> From whence come wars and fightings among you? come they not hence, even of your lusts that war in your members?

The word for *lusts* is actually "hedonism" or "pleasures." Struggles and conflicts within man and between men are the result of the overwhelming desire for pleasure that exists in the heart. There is nothing wrong with eating, drinking, marriage, and business pursuits, but when they become the chief pursuits of life instead of the knowledge of God, they cause spiritual insensitivity.

Violence in America and its Lack of Respect for Human Life

Documentation is not needed at this point as horrific mass murders in American society, as well as the legalization of abortion, have demonstrated the violence and lack of respect for human life that pervade modern society. Violence is also freely on display in movies and on television developing insensitivity in those who enjoy these means of entertainment.

The Corruption of a People of God

There was a corruption of human society in those ancient days when the "sons of God" married the "daughters of men."[1] Although there are various interpretations of this passage, its thrust is clear. Society was corrupted because of improper intermingling through marriage. If the interpretation is taken that the "sons of God" are the godly line of Seth, these marriages corrupted society through unequally yoked marriages of the godly line of Seth with heathen women. As marriage pictures a deeper spiritual picture of the relationship of God with His people, lack of fidelity to God, because of love for the world, has corrupted the present day church to the point that it has contributed to the moral corruption of society in general. The principle of Scripture is that light rejected brings greater darkness. It seems as though the Western world and America in particular, has come full circle in its rejection of biblical revelation. Countries in Europe that brought the Protestant Reformation now sit in spiritual darkness. The Protestant Reformation came to the shores of America from England through the Separatists and the Pilgrims as they settled the Northeastern Seaboard. Now America seems to be sinking into a moral malaise where the truth about God is being lost in the society at large.

The Crises in the Political and Economic Arena

Not only is there a crisis in the moral area in America, but there are crises in the political and the economic areas. Actually, these next two areas are a result of moral failure because morality extends into politics and economics. First, politically, America is continually on the move to a stronger central government and socialism. As people continue to look to government for solutions and depend on government for daily sustenance, the government will exert stronger control over them. Actually, stronger central government has been on the move since the Civil War when the North set up control over the South. The two world wars and the arrival of progressivism have steadily led to a stronger central government.[2] Second, economic problems at the time of this writing have led to an even stronger role of government with the economic "stimulus" and government involvement in banks and the auto industry. With America now over sixteen trillion dollars in debt (climbing daily), higher taxes, and a lower standard of living seem inevitable. It does not require a rocket scientist to see that America is presently on an unsustainable path to economic catastrophe. As the dollar weakens and other countries lose confidence in it, wild inflation is inevitable.

Bible Prophecy and the Decline of America

Although nations oftentimes do not pass off the scene as separate entities, they come to a place where they lose their power and influence. The fact that God deals with nations in judgment is evident in the Scriptures:

> The wicked shall be turned into hell [sheol], and all the nations that forget God (Psalm 9:17).

The economic trends in America fit Bible prophecy. The real power at the end of the age will be a Ten-Kingdom Federated Empire as predicted in the book of Revelation, possibly centered in the city of Rome.[3] Both America and Russia will fade in their world influence as the Antichrist gains power through control of a global economy. This control is made possible because world financial control has already come through the world monetary system. Relating to the prophesies of the control of the Antichrist over the wealth of the world, John Stormer states:[4]

> Consider these 2,500 year old prophesies in light of 1967 proposals for a world monetary system as the solution for the gold crisis[5] and a world banker who would control 'all gold and silver.' Consider these prophesies in light of proposals by UN Secretary General U Thant for world-wide redistribution of the wealth through a United Nations graduated income tax.

Russia and her allies will finally invade Israel and the Middle-East for a "spoil" since the Antichrist and his UN (Ten-Kingdoms) will have a strangle hold on the wealth of the Middle-East.

A new currency will be developed by this unified global power, which shall eventually turn into the "mark of the beast" spoken of in the book of Revelation.[6] Socialism is already the practical form of government in the European Union and is fast putting its tentacles on America indicating the trend to totalitarianism.

The Lessons Of History In Religious Past

The Cycle of Spiritual Revival

The history of America is similar to the individual Christian believer and Israel as recorded in the Old Testament. The Christian believer, individually, has a tendency to go through a cycle of spiritual rest to self-reliance and spiritual unrest, depending on whether he remains in fellowship with God. Israel in the Old Testament, especially in the book of Judges, went through periods of peace and rest to periods of defeat and unrest. For God's people, whenever circumstances seem advantageous and comfortable, the tendency is to rely on one's self rather than God. The same thing was true in the history of the people of God in the Old Testament. Whenever Israel became self-reliant, they went into bondage to a foreign power, and it took God-empowered judges to deliver them from bondage. Although America does not have the same status as a nation chosen by God such as Israel, it illustrates in its history the same spiritual vicissitudes.

Hope for America lies in hope for the individual as the individual is important to God. Although the Christian believer should be engaged in the political process, society

---

cannot be changed from the top down. It must be changed at the "grass roots" level through Christian believers who are living "Spirit-filled" lives.

A Panoramic Look at Revivals Preceding Times of Crisis

The First Great Awakening

America was founded in the crisis of the Revolutionary War. As England's tariffs and taxes on the colonies became more oppressive, in 1773 patriots, in defiance, tossed tons of tea overboard in the Boston Harbor-which came to be known as the "Boston Tea Party." The reaction of the British was to send troops to quell the rebellion, and the fight was on. Later, in 1776, at the Second Continental Congress, America declared its independence from England.

Before our country was founded, the early Separatists and Puritans that settled the Eastern Seaboard had a spiritual vitality and rigor established in the midst of the English persecution of religious dissidents and a harrowing trip over the Atlantic from England to America. Such great leaders as William Bradford, William Brewster, Richard Clyfton, and John Robinson were great spiritual leaders and expositors of the Bible.[1] Their preaching was like Ezra's of the Old Testament which exposited the Scripture and sought to interpret it with present application.

> So they read in the book in the law of God distinctly, and gave the sense, and caused them to understand the reading (Nehemiah 8:8).

Before the strain of the Revolutionary War, the First Great Awakening, a Christian revival, took place in America from 1720-1760. This revival unified the country and prepared the colonists for revolution, while bringing a Protestant Christian consensus to bear upon the minds of the framers of our constitution. Although not all of our early leaders were Christians in the Bible sense (i.e. Thomas Jefferson was a fledgling deist) they acknowledged God as they sought to found a nation based on laws.

The Need for a Spiritual Revival

Practical Bible exposition always accompanies spiritual vitality and revival. However, as a new generation arose in the colonies, more ministers went into the ministry without a conversion experience, and preaching became dry doctrinal treatises that did not hold much interest for the man in the pew. Consequently church attendance and the interest in spiritual things shifted to survival in the colonies. In order to attract people to the church the "half way" covenant was developed. This agreement allowed people to become members without a profession of faith. Children of church members were also allowed to become members because they were participators in the "covenant." They allowed these children to receive baptism but not the Lord's Table or to vote. Without a biblical experience of conversion religion became dead and lifeless, and there was little evangelism in the colonies.

Leaders and Results of the Revival

The first spark of spiritual Christian revival came among the Dutch speaking people of New Jersey. In 1720 Theodore Jacob Frelinghuysen, a German-born, Dutch-educated minister, came to minister to the Dutch settlement in the Raritan River Valley. He combined preaching for commitment, reading of English Puritan literature, warning about religious formalism, and the need for conversion. One of his converts was Gilbert Tennent, who with his sons became leaders and evangelists in the First Great Awakening. Perhaps the most well-known leader in this Great Awakening was the pastor at Northampton, MA., Jonathan Edwards. Edwards seemed to be a throwback to early Puritan leaders in America as he preached with great wisdom and conviction about "licentious living" and "self-reliance" which he said came about through the doctrines of Arminianism. He was also a prolific writer who produced such works as "Sinners in the Hand of an Angry God"[2] and a work that influenced other ministers toward revival entitled, *A Faithful Narrative of a Surprising Work of God in the Conversion of Many Hundreds of Souls in North Hampton.*[3] The man who united the colonies in these revivals was the English evangelist George Whitfield. As he traveled throughout the colonies, Whitfield preached the gospel with much authority and power. He was blessed with a moving eloquent oratory that was delivered with great volume to crowds who came to hear him. The results of the revival were numerous. The tide of apostasy was turned by confronting the problem of unconverted ministers and church members, and many of them experienced genuine conversion. The revivals emphasized holiness and restored a pure church. Also, at this time, many educational institutions were established to train ministers and provide a Bible-based education. For example, the Log College was established by William Tennent, which was the forerunner of Princeton. The College of Philadelphia was the forerunner of the University of Pennsylvania. Liberty Hall was the forerunner of Washington and Lee University. Kings College in New York was established, which later became Columbia University. The College of Rhode Island, in Providence, became Brown University. Queens College in New Brunswick, New Jersey was the forerunner of Rutgers. However, these institutions have become overwhelmingly secular today.

The Second Great Awakening

The Second Great Awakening in America lasted from about 1775 to 1840. As the nation moved westward, revivals were led by such preachers from Kentucky as James McGready and Barton Stone. At the same time spiritual infidelity had crept into the colleges established in the First Great Awakening along the Eastern Seaboard. Timothy Dwight, the grandson of Jonathan Edwards and president of Yale University, led a revival at Yale College. He preached to the Yale students, interspersing doctrinal teaching with emotional calls to repentance, which led to Christian revivals on campus. He argued against deism and skepticism which had already become fashionable among intellectuals during the time of the Revolution.

The Businessmen's Prayer Revival

The third nationwide revival took place between 1857-1859. This has been called the Businessman's Prayer Revival. Prayer meetings began at the Fulton Street Dutch Reformed Church in New York City and spread to other cities in America such as Philadelphia, Boston, Chicago, and Atlanta. Infidelity to the Word of God was rampant before these revival prayer meetings began as a materialistic outlook began to shape America during the Industrial Revolution. Many people were converted during this time and the tide of unbelief and infidelity was slowed. By the time of the outbreak of the crisis of the Civil War in 1861, Americans had been blessed with periods of Christian revival, and they were spiritually prepared for the ravages that the Civil War would bring upon the churches in America.

The Businessman's Prayer Revival not only prepared the nation for the crisis of the Civil War but it also had far reaching effects that touched the last half of the nineteenth century until the modern day. This revival was the last major nation-wide Christian revival to occur in America.

1. It raised up great Christian evangelists and leaders such as D. L. Moody and George Needham. Needham was affected by a nearly simultaneous revival in Ulster, Ireland and then became involved in the US revival.

2. It prepared the American religious world by confronting the crisis of religious liberalism, which is the parent of political liberalism. Religious liberalism denies the literal interpretation of the Bible, the total depravity and inherent sinfulness of man, and advocates a social gospel that proposes that society can be changed through church and government intervention. It also champions Darwinism and evolution, and applies it to religion by advocating the inherent progress of man to perfection. Religious liberalism also proposes a higher criticism of the Bible by denying the historicity of the Bible, the possibility of miracles, and by denying the uniqueness of Christianity among religions and the uniqueness of Jesus Christ. Before the crisis of liberalism actually reached the shores of America from Germany and England, God raised up this third awakening, not only to prepare the nation for the Civil War, but to prepare it for the religious and political liberalism which spawned philosophies such

as nazism, socialism, and communism all of which brought two world wars and the "cold war" in its train. Religious liberalism still exists in the twenty-first century and expresses itself through larger church and government roles in the societal problems of man. The answer to religious liberalism was born in the Bible and Prophetic Conference Movement, which took place between 1878 and 1914. These conferences began in New York City, which was the first of five major conferences; the last one took place at the Moody church in Chicago. Leaders in these conferences and those influenced by these leaders began the Bible institute and Christian college movements in the early twentieth century. This was in response to the crisis of religious liberalism, which had entered into America's mainline protestant Christian denominations and into its Christian colleges and seminaries.[4]

3. It produced many conversions as well as a groundswell of evangelism and missions that went beyond the borders of America.

4. It also had an indirect affect on the production of the *Scofield Reference Bible*. Alwyn Ball, Jr. and his friend Frances E. Fitch still conducted noon prayer meetings in the New York Financial District- the place where the prayer meeting revivals started in 1857. Ball, along with another business man, John T. Pirie, were financial sponsors of the *Scofield Reference Bible* that is still beloved by many believers today.[5]

The Decline of a Nation

Even though Christianity still has influence on the "grass roots" level, America is again in moral decline and in need of a spiritual revival. Author James Black touches on the subject of the reasons for the decline of a nation.[6]

> [The reasons] included over-centralized government, inordinate growth of taxation, a top heavy system of administration, promotion of the wrong people, the urge to overspend, and the rise of 'liberal opinion'— that is, the popularization of attitudes and policies controlled by sentiment rather than sound moral judgment.

Although the exact source of the following has been questioned, democracies seem to move through a cycle from spiritual faith to dependence and bondage. A democracy cannot exist as a permanent form of government. It can only exist until the voters discover that they can vote themselves largesse from the public treasury. From that moment on, the majority always votes for the candidates promising the most benefits from the public treasury resulting in a democracy which collapses over loose fiscal policy and becomes a dictatorship. The average age of the world's greatest civilizations has been 200 years. There seems to be the course of democracy from a great beginning to a spiritual decline. Democracies move through a cycle from spiritual faith to bondage:[7]

Spiritual Faith to Courage;
Courage to Freedom;
Freedom to Abundance;
Abundance to Selfishness;
Selfishness to Complacency;
Complacency to Apathy;
Apathy to Fear;
Fear to Dependency;
Dependency to Bondage.

What does a Spiritual Revival Look Like?

> Wherefore he saith, Awake thou that sleepest, and
> arise from the dead, and Christ shall give thee light
> (Ephesians 5:14).

An individual or nation needs revival when it becomes complacent and content with itself and the status quo.

In a Context of Family Relationships

The admonition to *awake from sleep* is to Christian believers, who may be slumbering spiritually; it comes in the context of a description of the Spirit-filled life and family relationships.[8] The failure to pass on a zeal for God and a dedication to Christ to the next generation will in itself bring a need for Christian revival. Even a cursory look at the Old Testament will show that such godly men as King David and the prophet Samuel had profligate and wicked children. One of the signs of a Christian revival will be a Spirit-filled love of God which will express itself in family relationships. This will occur before the end of the age and the coming of the "Day of the Lord."

> Behold, I will send you Elijah the prophet before the
> coming of the great and dreadful day of the LORD, And he
> shall turn the heart of the fathers to the children, and the
> heart of the children to their fathers, lest I come and smite
> the earth with a curse (Malachi 4:5-6).

Some of the characteristics of the Last Days will be that ". . . men will be lovers of their own selves . . . and without natural affection . . ."[9] Selfish living in families will cause alienation in affection even among family members. One of the phenomenon of the past century has been the breakup of the family with divorce and the absence of either a father or a mother in the family household. In fact, some mental health experts think "parental alienation" should be an official psychological diagnosis in the updated *Diagnostic and Statistical Manual of Mental Disorders*, the "bible" of diagnosis released 2012.[10] Statistics show that among children who live with only one parent, whether because of divorce or separation, 8.3 million live with their mothers and just 1.4 million with their dads."[11] The absence of a father figure can be disastrous to the nurture of a child. These verses in Proverbs 30:11-14 could well describe this generation:

> There is a generation that curseth their father, and doth not bless their mother. There is a generation that are pure in their own eyes, and yet is not washed from their filthiness. There is a generation, O how lofty are their eyes! And their eyelids are lifted up. There is a generation, whose teeth are like swords, and their jaw teeth like knives, to devour the poor from off the earth, and the needy from among men.

Here a generation is described in the Last Days that are without parental affection, without a sense of sin and shame, prideful and violent. Believing parents best illustrate Spirit-filled love for their children when they teach them the love for and fear of the Lord as shown in Deuteronomy 6:4-7:

> Hear, O, Israel: The LORD our God is one LORD: And thou shalt love the LORD thy God with all thine heart, and with all thy soul and with all thy might. And these words, which I command thee this day, shall be in thine heart; And thou shalt teach them diligently unto thy children, and shall talk of them when thou sittest in thine house, and when thou

walkest by the way, and when thou liest down, and when thou risest up.

This responsibility to instruct our children is also emphasized for the Christian church of the New Testament. The admonition is addressed to fathers in Ephesians 6:4:

And, ye fathers, provoke not your children to wrath: but bring them up in the nurture and admonition of the Lord.

If parents discipline their children through love and the fear of the Lord, they will raise young people who are neither angry nor saddled with depression. The admonition to bring up children "in the nurture and admonition of the Lord" comes in the context of teaching about the Spirit-filled life as it involves family relationships such as a husband's love for his wife, her submission to her husband, and obedience of children to their parents.[12] In other words, the most important service a Christian believer can give his Lord is to love and spiritually nourish his family, and this can only be accomplished through the power of the Holy Spirit. Zeal for the spiritual commitment and spiritual growth of our children will characterize a Spirit-filled life and Christian revival. As a glance is taken of Christian revivals in the history of America there are many other manifestations that characterize revivals.

A Concern for Evangelism and Missions

A concern for evangelism and missions was an outgrowth of all of the Great Awakenings. Many people were genuinely born-again and were concerned about others who need Christ, while they dedicated themselves to the great missionary enterprise.

Great Leaders

A Spiritual revival always has had great leaders who had a zeal for God and a commitment to the mission of God to reach others with the gospel of Christ. God raised up such great leaders in history as Jonathan Edwards, George Whitfield, William Tennent, Timothy Dwight, and, as a result of the prayer revival, D. L. Moody.

Prayer

Earnest prayer is always a key element of a moving of the Spirit in spiritual revival. The Businessmen's Prayer Meeting Revival that swept America produced evangelists such as D. L. Moody and the Great Mission Movement of the late nineteenth and early twentieth century.

Respect of and Desire for God

A renewed respect, fear, and love for God Himself always characterized revival, replacing the fear of man. A new desire for holiness and a thirst for God Himself also characterized the revivals of the past, replacing self-satisfaction and self-reliance.

Teaching and Preaching for Commitment

Expository Bible teaching and preaching with application characterized the early Christian Separatists from England in the colonies, and they were also found in the Christian revivals in the history of America. It was a preaching for commitment that moved scores of people to commit themselves to Christ and the pursuit of God. Revivals in the past stemmed the tide of the departure from truth in America and fortified believers in that truth.

Revivals Begin with Individuals

The hour is late, but there is always hope for a renewal of repentance toward God and faith in Jesus Christ in America. However, spiritual revival begins with individuals and individual leaders. The spiritual revival led by Ezra and Nehemiah in the Old Testament, as recorded in their books, is instructive for America and the individual believer in this modern day. Israel and Judah had gone into captivity to Assyria and Babylon respectively but now, in response to the prayers of the people of God, the edict of Cyrus, the king of Persia, Ezra, and Nehemiah returned to Jerusalem to rebuild the city and repair the walls. America has now gone into captivity to the enemies of moral relativism, big government, and economic servitude in society in general as well as spiritual apostasy and coldness in the organized Christian church in particular. In addition to these things, America has increasingly aligned itself with the New World Order by working through the UN and possesses the possibility of going into servitude to the New World Order. However, the example of the spiritual revival led by Ezra and Nehemiah illustrates that it is never too late for spiritual revival.

The Characteristics Of The Spiritual Revival Led By Ezra And Nehemiah

Effect on the Leaders

Humbled Themselves

This spiritual revival was characterized by the prayers of repentance of its leadership. Ezra and Nehemiah did not view themselves as being aloof from the general condition of the people but rather identified themselves as part of the nation needing revival. Notice the plural *we* in the following passage of Scripture:

> And it came to pass, when I heard these words, that I sat down and wept, and mourned certain days, and fasted, and prayed before the God of heaven, And said, I beseech thee, O LORD God of heaven, the great and terrible [awe-inspiring] God, who keepeth covenant and mercy for them that love him and observe his commandments: Let thine ear now be attentive, and thine eyes open, that thou mayest hear the prayer of thy servant, which I pray before thee

now, day and night, for the children of Israel thy servants, and confess the sins of the children of Israel, which *we* [italics mine] have sinned against thee: both I and my father's house have sinned. *We* have dealt very corruptly against thee, and have not kept the commandments, nor the statutes, nor the judgments [ordinances], which thou commandest thy servant Moses (Nehemiah 1:4-7).

As Nehemiah offered this prayer of repentance, in which he magnified the greatness and mercy of God, he recognized that he needed to lead in this intercessory prayer for Israel by confessing his own sins as well as the sins of the people.

Had a Vision

These leaders had a spiritual vision for revival, repentance, and restoration. They had a vision of what God would be able to do with a people who would be right with Him. They will encourage and strengthen the people to action in the face of distressing circumstances as seen in Nehemiah 2:17-18:

Then said I unto them, Ye see the distress that we are in, how Jerusalem lieth waste, and the gates thereof are burned with fire: come, and let us build up the wall of Jerusalem, that we be no more a reproach. Then I told them of the hand of my God which was good upon me; and also the king's words that he had spoken unto me. And they said, Let us rise up and build. So they strengthened their hands for this good work.

Nehemiah motivated the people to action through his testimony of how God was at work in this endeavor.

Stood up to Resistance

A spiritual revival requires a willingness to work in spite of resistance from enemies. As revival accompanied by a Spirit-filled life comes, the enemies of God are going to be there to resist it. The believers in the days of Ezra and Nehemiah kept persevering despite mocking and ridicule by the inhabitants of the land. Also, they continued to build despite an active conspiracy against them.

> But it came to pass, that when Sanballat heard that we builded the wall, he was wroth, and took great indignation, and mocked the Jews . . . But it came to pass, that when Sanballat, and Tobiah, and the Arabians, and the Ammonites, and the Ashdodites, heard that the walls of Jerusalem were made up, and that the breaches began to be stopped, then they were very wroth, And conspired all of them together to come and to fight against Jerusalem, and to hinder it (Nehemiah 4:1, 7-8).

Effect on the People

Discernment and Application of the Word of God

Ezra was the leader in this desire to know the Word of God and to practice it. Therefore he prepared his heart for this noble task.

> For Ezra had prepared his heart to seek the law of the LORD, and to do it, and to teach in Israel statutes and judgments (Ezra 7:10).

Expository and practical Bible preaching by the leaders accompanied the revival under Ezra and Nehemiah with the result that the people gained spiritual discernment as we see in Nehemiah 8:8:

> So they read in the book in the law of God distinctly, and gave the sense, and caused them to understand the reading.

Explanation and application of the Word of God helped the people to discern how the Word of God applied to their present situation. In fact, according to Luke discernment is not present unless there is the obedience to the Word of God:

> But that on the good ground are they, which, in an honest and good heart, having heard the word, keep it, and bring forth fruit with patience (Luke 8:15).

Obedience Prompted by Faith

The revival under Ezra and Nehemiah was characterized by obedience prompted by faith in the Word of God.

> Who is there among you of all his people? his God be with him, and let him go up to Jerusalem, which is in Judah, and build the house of the LORD God of Israel, (he is the God,) which is in Jerusalem (Ezra 1:3).

The response to the Word received from the Lord and a consciousness of His presence was to go up to rebuild the temple of Jerusalem. Obedience to the Lord was demonstrated by the Jews in all areas such as reforming the priesthood, keeping the sacrifices, the feasts, and the Sabbath as well as rejecting mixed marriages with the heathen in the land.[1]

Heartfelt Recognition of the Greatness of God

A heartfelt recognition of the greatness of God resulting in a genuine worship of God accompanied the revival under Ezra and Nehemiah.

> Then were assembled unto me everyone that trembled at the words of the God of Israel, because of the transgression of those that had been carried away; and I sat astonied [appalled] until the evening sacrifice (Ezra 9:4).

This heartfelt recognition of the greatness of God resulted in both worship and praise to the Lord. The Levites began to recognize the greatness and awesome nature of God:

> Stand up and bless the LORD your God for ever and ever; and blessed be thy glorious name, which is exalted above all blessing and praise. Thou, even thou, art LORD alone; thou hast made heaven, the heaven of heavens, with all their host, the earth, and all things that are there in, the seas, and all that is therein, and thou preservest them all; and the host of heaven worshippeth thee (Nehemiah 9:32).

God was recognized as being great, mighty, and faithful to His covenant with His people.

> Now therefore, our God, the great, the mighty, and the terrible [awe inspiring] God, who keepeth covenant and mercy, let not all this trouble seem little before thee, that hath come upon us, on our kings, on our princes, and on our priests, and on our prophets, and on our fathers, and on all thy people, since the times of the kings of Assyria unto this day.[2]

The people recognized the justice of God in dealing with them and implored God on the basis of His greatness and faithfulness as they renewed the vow of their covenant to Him. Lest the people become swallowed up during their repentance and sorrow for their sin, Nehemiah reminds them that "the joy of the LORD is your strength."

> And Nehemiah, which is the Tirshatha, and Ezra the priest and scribe, and the Levites that taught the people, said unto all the people, This day is holy unto the LORD, your God; mourn not, nor weep. For all the people wept, when they heard the words of the law. Then he said unto them, Go your way, eat the fat, and drink the sweet, and send portions unto them for whom nothing is prepared: for this day is holy unto our LORD: Neither be ye sorry [grieved]; for the joy of the LORD is your strength (Nehemiah 8:9-10).

They recognized their "spiritual roots" and how they as a people had strayed away from fidelity to their God. The people recounted their origin: their rescue from Egypt, provision in the wilderness, and the many times they forgot the Lord by becoming involved in spiritual infidelity.[3] They departed from the basic commands of the law such as the command to love, fear, obey, and to cling (cleave) to Him.[4] America is in trouble because she has moved away from the heritage of her spiritual roots as a nation founded upon the laws of God. When a nation or individual strays from his Christian heritage, a return to his spiritual roots through repentance is necessary. Author James Nelson Black points out that religion was "always foundational to the great societies."[5] How much more is that true of America which had a Christian influence at its founding. There comes a time when there is a need to return to God through repentance, which involves a wholehearted fear and love for God, resulting in obedience to Him.

— 6 —

Rebellion: In The Mystery Form Of The Kingdom

The age old question which has occupied philosophers' thinking throughout the epochs of history is how a good God could allow human suffering and evil in His kingdom. Furthermore, if God was really in charge, could He not change things immediately? Certainly He could at any time forcefully quash the rebellion in His kingdom and end the evil and the suffering in the world. There is a future day when He will end all rebellion by putting down all His enemies and the enemies of real peace and reconciliation upon the earth.[1] God rules at the present time in the mystery form of His kingdom. It is evident that even though great empires seem to exert wicked control over mankind, it is God who both sets up kingdoms and brings them to termination. King Nebuchadnezzar of the Great Babylonian Empire was told he would be humbled through a mighty act of God until he would "know that the most High ruleth in the kingdom of men, and giveth it to whomsoever he will."[2] The mystery form of the kingdom is the sowing of the seed of the gospel of Christ while wickedness exists among men. It is also God gathering His people while rebellion exists among men. The removal of evil and rebellion will eventually take place when Christ returns to judge the nations and Israel, and set up His kingdom over the earth.[3] However, before Christ returns He is calling out a people to prepare for His kingdom.[4] Actually, this is the only explanation of why God allows evil and suffering to continue at this present time. God is giving man the opportunity through belief in the gospel to enter the future paradise of His kingdom. The only reason for the delay in his coming is His desire that all men would come to Him for eternal salvation.[5]

The Original Rebellion of Lucifer and Man

Somewhere in the distant past before the creation of man one of the choice angels of God, called Lucifer, rebelled against his subservient position by desiring to be "like the Most High."[6] He was the "anointed cherub that covereth," possibly the head of a select group of angels called the Cherubim. Bible revelation declares that his sins were pride with the desire for independent autonomy.[7] It was the same temptation he offered in the Garden of Eden when the serpent said, ". . . ye shall be as gods, knowing good and evil."[8] Today, because of the fall of man, although man is not sovereign over his own destiny and future, he has the same satanic desire to be independent from his creator and the same spirit of pride and independence from God.[9]

Satan's Rebellion in the End Times

Just as Satan introduced rebellion in the kingdom of God at the beginning of time, both in the heavenlies among the angels and on earth among men, he will introduce increased rebellion among the nations at the end of the age. Now Satan is the "prince of the power of the air" in that his activities take place both in the heavens and on the earth. As the "accuser of the brethren," he now even has access, by permission of God, to the heaven where God dwells to accuse the saints.[10] However, Satan will be cast down to the earth after a final attempt to dethrone God and His angels. This event will likely occur in the middle of the Tribulation period when Satan will enter into the Antichrist who then sets himself up as God in human flesh.[11] The fact that the Antichrist is supernaturally energized is indicated by the fact that he ascends from the bottomless pit which is literally "the Abyss."[12] The Antichrist then will declare himself to be god and Armageddon will follow. Armageddon is not a single battle but a campaign.[13] World War III will ensue among nations culminating in the nations rebelling against God Himself. The prophet Daniel speaks of nations in conflict at the end of the last half of the Tribulation. He is speaking of the Antichrist in this prophetic context:

> But tidings out of the east and out of the north shall trouble him: therefore he shall go forth with great fury to destroy, and utterly to make [sweep] away many. And he shall plant the tabernacles of his palace between the seas in the glorious holy mountain; yet he shall come to his end, and none shall help him (Daniel 11:44-45).

The Alignment of Nations in the Modern Day which Foreshadows the Rebellion in the End Times

A Revival of an Imperial Roman Empire (The West)

This final alignment of nations, in the Last Days, is a continuation of the Roman Empire because the feet and ten toes are considered an extension of the old Roman Empire by the prophet Daniel:

> And the fourth kingdom shall be strong as iron: forasmuch as iron breaketh in pieces and subdueth all things: and as iron that breaketh all these, shall it break in pieces and bruise. And whereas thou sawest the feet and toes, part of potters' clay, and part of iron, the kingdom shall be divided; but there shall be in it of the strength of the iron, forasmuch as thou sawest the iron mixed with miry clay. And as the toes of the feet were part of iron, and part of clay, so the kingdom shall be partly strong, and partly broken (Daniel 2:40-42).

Dwight Pentecost in *Things to Come* states:

> The final form of Gentile power is an outgrowth from and final development of the Fourth Great Empire, the Roman. This final form is represented by the feet and ten toes (319).

Although the imperial form of the Roman Empire ended in 476 AD, it will be restored under the Antichrist. In light of Scripture, the Roman Empire has never actually ceased to exist. Its influence continues to this present day. First of all, fragments of the Roman Empire continue to exist separately as nations in the Western world today. Secondly, the Roman Catholic Church has maintained its influence in politics to this day. Thirdly, Latin continues to be the language used in jurisprudence and science today. Lastly, the legal codes which protect individual rights and property in many European countries and in America are based on Roman law.

This revived imperial form of the Roman Empire will more than likely include the United States, the United

Kingdom, and nations from the European Continent. The final Ten-Kingdom Federated Empire under the Antichrist will come out of these areas. This is already foreshadowed by the present European Union.

Presently the US has troops stationed around the world. The Iraq and Afghanistan wars were led by the western segment of the UN largely supplied by US firepower. The help to overthrow brutal dictator Gaddafi was supplied by the UN in turn largely supplied by US firepower. Although Republican Presidential candidate Ron Paul correctly pointed out the dangers of undeclared preemptive war, this trend will be part of the revived Roman Empire neo-democracy of the Last Days. There will be a short lived pax-Romona or pax-Europa in the world for the first half of the Tribulation period which is three and a half years. Because of a global economy even Russia and China shall acquiesce for a time to the rise of the Antichrist. The Antichrist will arise because of a world crisis and the Rapture could certainly qualify as a crisis. An economic and moral crisis already exists, but a deeper chaos could ensue due to the Rapture.

Russia (the King of the North)

Daniel 11: 44 speaks of an invasion of Russia to challenge the Antichrist at the end of the Tribulation as all nations converge on Jerusalem. This is not the same invasion as the invasion by Russia and Iran and other allies against Israel. The first invasion will probably occur just before the first half of the Tribulation ends. This first invasion is recorded in Ezekiel 38:1-6b:

> And the word of the LORD came to me, saying, Son
> of man, set thy face against Gog, the land of Magog,
> the chief prince of Meshech and Tubal and prophesy

against him, And say, Thus saith, God: Behold, I am against thee, O Gog, the chief prince of Meshech and Tubal, And I will turn thee back, and put hooks into thy jaws, and I will bring thee forth, and all thine army, horses, and horsemen, all of them clothed with all sorts of armor, even a great company with bucklers and shields, all of them handling swords; Persia, Cush, and Put [Ethiopia and Libya] with them: all of them with shields and helmet; Gomer, and all its hordes; . . . and many people with thee.

This is an invasion of Israel by Russia (called by the ancient name Magog) and a group of nations including African and Muslim nations such as Iran. Until 1932 Iran was called by its ancient name Persia.[14]

The time of the invasion

This invasion will occur after Israel is gathered in her land. Ezekiel's vision of the dry and dead bones which resurrect into a live body pictures the gathering of Israel to a homeland. Israel had been scattered among Gentile nations since the destruction of Jerusalem in 70 AD. This gathering as a nation took place in 1948 under the Balfour declaration.[15] More specifically, the invasion will occur when Israel is dwelling in "unwalled villages, dwelling safely." Therefore, this invasion still remains in the future.

And thou shalt say, I will go up in the land of unwalled villages; I will go to them that are at rest, that dwell safely, all of them dwelling without walls, and having neither bars nor gates (Ezekiel 38:11).

This certainly cannot take place in Israel today as she is surrounded by avowed enemies such as Syria and Iran and feels the need to defend herself. It will be true after the Antichrist makes a covenant to protect Israel from all enemies at the beginning of the Tribulation.

The invasion will probably occur at the middle of the Tribulation because it will result in the Antichrist moving into a power vacuum, created by the demise of Russia. Near the second coming of Christ, Russia will regroup to again challenge the Antichrist. The Antichrist will enter into Israel, declaring himself to be God, simultaneously probably taking credit for the defeat of Russia. It will also be the beginning of a national Jewish conversion:

> And I will set My glory among the nations, and all the nations shall see My judgment that I have executed, and My hand that I have laid on them. So the house of Israel shall know that I am the LORD their God from that day forward (Ezekiel 39:21-22 New King James Version).

God is the One who will supernaturally destroy Russia and its group of allies, but He may also use firepower from other nations as they battle over dwindling energy supplies in the world. "Calling for a sword" suggests intermediate agency and "every man's sword shall be against his brother" may not represent confusion but the beginning of a worldwide nuclear conflagration.[16] Nuclear warfare would be followed by pestilence and disturbances in the atmosphere. This could be signified by "the overflowing rain."[17] Certainly other nations, including the West, know that Russia has "come to take a spoil"[18] Yet, even if an intermediate agency is used, it is ultimately God who is responsible for the defeat of Russia.

The reason for the invasion

The reason for the invasion is clearly stated in Ezekiel 38:12:

> To take a spoil, and to take a prey; to turn thy hand upon
> the desolate places that are now inhabited, and upon the
> people that are gathered out of the nations, which have
> gotten cattle and goods, that dwell in the midst of the land.

While Israel is dwelling safely, she has grown wealthy. The purpose of the invasion is to destroy Israel and gain a stranglehold on the wealth and oil resources left in the world. Although Russia, as well as the US, is rich in oil and natural gas resources, they lack the money or refuse to extract the oil from their own countries.[19] Green energy simply cannot supply the burgeoning industrial populations of the world. Current events illustrate that Russia supplies arms and support to Iran and Syria and do not support militarily and economically the efforts of the western segment of the UN in the Arab world.[20] They have their own economic interests to protect and do not view sanctions on Iran favorably. Russia remains the *Bear* and eventually will act according to Bible prophecy to protect its interests in the world.

The result of the invasion

Russia and the nations who will move against Israel will meet their "waterloo." The anger of God against them will be supremely demonstrated in this judgment of Gog and Magog as recorded in Ezekiel 39:1-6:

> Therefore, thou son of man, prophesy against Gog, and
> say, Thus saith the Lord GOD; Behold, I am against thee,

O Gog, the chief prince of Meshech and Tubal: And I will turn thee back, and leave but the sixth part of thee, and will cause thee to come up from the north parts, and will bring thee upon the mountains of Israel: And I will smite thy bow out of thy left hand, and will cause thine arrows to fall out of thy right hand. Thou shalt fall upon the mountains of Israel, thou, and all thy bands, and the peoples that is with thee; I will give thee unto the ravenous birds of every sort, and to the beasts of the field to be devoured. Thou shalt fall upon the open field: for I have spoken it, saith the Lord GOD. And I will send a fire on Magog, and among them that dwell carelessly in the isles: and they shall know that I am the LORD.

The Kings of the East (China and Other Nations in the Orient)

But tidings out of the east and out of the north shall trouble him . . . (Daniel 11:44a).

And the sixth angel poured out his vial upon the great river Euphrates; and the water thereof was dried up, that the way of the kings of the east might be prepared (Revelation 16:12).

And the four angels were loosed, which were prepared for an hour, and a day, and a month, and a year, for to slay the third part of man. And the number of the army of horseman was two hundred thousand thousand and I heard the number of them (Revelation 9:15-16).

These are the oriental hordes, led by China, who could easily field an army of 200 million. A development in modern times is the rise of China on the world industrial and global economic scene. This invasion seems to take place at end of the campaign of Armageddon as the kings of the East jockey for position to protect their own interests on the world scene.[21]

The Removal of the Spirit = Demonic Energy to Rebellion

The gathering of the oriental hordes, as well as the king of the North, in the Holy Land to battle the Antichrist is demonically energized.

> And I saw three unclean spirits like frogs come out of the mouth of the dragon, and out of the mouth of the beast, and out of the mouth of the false prophet. For they are the spirits of devils [demons], working miracles, which go forth unto the kings of the earth, and of the whole world, to gather them to the battle of the great day of God Almighty (Revelation 16:13-14).

Contrast that to the church age of today when the Holy Spirit is restraining sin. As the kings of the earth converge against each other in the Holy Land, Christ appears in heaven and the kings seek to fight against Him as recorded in Revelation 19:19-20:

> And I saw the beast, and the kings of the earth, and their armies, gathered together to make war against him that sat on the horse, and against his army. And the beast was taken, and with him the false prophet that wrought miracles before him, with which he deceived them that had received the mark of the beast, and them that worshipped his image. These both were cast alive into a lake of fire burning with brimstone.

If this futile effort to fight against Christ seems fantastic and fanciful, remember that people are by nature rebels against a Holy God. All this rebellion will be graphically and dramatically openly on display at the battle of Armageddon.

—7—

The Rise Of A
Neo-Democracy

The Final Form of Autocratic Government

The next autocratic form of government to arise at the end of the age is neo-democracy. A neo-democracy element is presently rising through the western segment of the UN which will become a strong central government out of which the Antichrist will arise. This neo-democracy will fulfill Daniel's prophecy of a government of iron mixed with clay which will seek to mix autocratic and democratic elements.[1] People eventually seem to elect the leaders they deserve and desire. If society in general moves away from moral absolutes into moral relativism, they will elect a leader who is moved by lawless ambition and pragmatism instead of truth. As people look more to government for answers, they will choose a leader and support him because he seems to represent what they themselves desire. Therefore, in this neo-democracy, this leader will *not* have to seek control through force and armaments. The desperate crises in the world will cause the general populace to willingly support him. This neo-democracy is a natural companion to socialism as the democratic element cries for the power of the people and equality. Yet this equality is not maintained in practicality and experience as certain people seem to rise to the top economically. In order to maintain this equality, the government must step in to "redistribute" the wealth.[2]

Neo-democracy as the Power of the State

This neo-democracy will have a dialectical mixture of democracy and socialism which will eventually resemble communism because it will result in statism or autocracy. The neo-democracy sweeping the world today, as seen in the Middle East and Russia, does not have the foundation of the democracy which exists in our constitutional American republic. Our founders wanted a government based on laws which can only proceed from the lawgiver himself, who is God. Our laws in America today are still based largely on the Judeo-Christian ethic. The individual is more important than the state or the community because governments will pass away, but the soul is eternal. When words are used like "the world order" and the "world community," the state rather than the individual is viewed as being all important. Although there are many viable democracies in the world today, true freedom can only come when man can govern himself. This self-governing can only genuinely come from an inward power supplied by God Himself.[3] As a populace becomes lawless the result will be autocratic control. As the Soviet Union fell in the latter part of the twentieth century, Russia seemed to be moving from communism to democracy. Russia was controlled, in its past history, by czars and communism. They do not have the same foundation for democracy as America which was founded, at least partially, in the framework of a Christian Protestant tradition. This tradition resulted in a constitution based upon law rather than the whims of a monarch or a changing society.[4] The Russian people tired of the malaise and lawlessness that occurred in the "democracy" that emerged in Russia. The result was that President Putin became a more autocratic leader. At the time of this writing, he has been elected again as prime minister. At the time of this writing longtime dictators such as Anwar Sadat of Egypt and Colonel Gaddafi of Libya have recently been overthrown in the Middle East in the name of democratic rule in the so-called "Arab spring." As in the case of Russia, there has been no real foundation for democracy in the past in the Middle East, and the sad result of the clamoring for democracy will be the rising of a "strongman" to "enforce" it. This call for democracy will result in a neo-democracy. This, in turn, will result in an enforced peace pact by the West upon Israel and the Arab world. Actually, the involvement of the West in the Middle East is nothing new in history. The League of Nations partitioned Israel and Palestine between Britain and France after the dissolution of the Ottoman Empire.[5]

Moving to Central Government

In order for this Middle East settlement to take place, America will have to continue to move further away from its founding ideals for individual freedom while following the same path that Europe has taken toward a strong central government. The crisis in America is great because of religious and moral failure. There is a generation rising that does not recognize our unique Christian heritage and which will increasingly look for answers from the government because of economic decline. Logic would tell us that the hour is later than ever before and that this downward course of spiritual and moral decline must be reversed, in order for America to continue as an influential nation on the world scene.

The Unexpected Great Event

The Appearance of Peace, Safety, and then, Sudden Destruction

> The lord of that servant shall come in a day when he
> looketh not for him, and in an hour that he is not aware
> of (Matthew 24:50).

> For yourselves know perfectly that the day of the Lord
> so cometh as a thief in the night. For when they shall say,
> Peace and safety; then sudden destruction cometh upon
> them, as travail upon a woman with child; and they shall
> not escape (1 Thessalonians 5:2-3).

The Day of the Lord will come as a "thief in the night" to the
world because they do not believe on Christ. Furthermore,
the second coming of Christ will occur when the leaders of
the world seem to have gained control of some of their most
thorny problems such as the Middle East dilemma and the
economic crisis.

The great power of the Last Days, unlike the situation
which existed in the twentieth century when the US and Russia
were the dominant world powers, will be the Ten Kingdom

Federated Alliance over which the Antichrist rises to rule. The Antichrist will rise to power through a neo-democracy in which the people willingly give him authority to rule because the crises in the world seem to leave no other option. He will also preside over a settlement of the continually vexing Middle East crisis between Arabs and Jews through a covenant made for seven years. The world, at the beginning of the Tribulation period, will seem to enter an unparalleled era of peace. There will be an apparent settlement of the Middle East problem between Israel and the Arabs, a political and economic union and an apparent world nuclear disarmament. Russia and China, at least for a time, will acquiesce in the interest of self-preservation for economic survival.[1] This pseudo peace will be destroyed because of the invasion by Russia and her allies against Israel. After this, the nations will be in conflict and converge on Jerusalem. Then Christ will return to execute the sudden destruction of His wrath upon the armies of the world.

The Modern Day Movement toward Unity

The modern day already illustrates that the world is heading into a unity and solidarity that has never been experienced in its past history:

1. Technological advancements made possible by the computer are setting the stage for world-wide control.
2. The horror of total world destruction through a nuclear war among nations and the lessons of the devastation of two world wars have brought a new urgency to diplomatic efforts and talk of disarmament.
3. The economic solidarity of nations, as the world is now in a global economy, is a motivator to diplomatic efforts.

One should not assume that all leaders in this present age have sinister motivations for world control. The modern world, being a creation from past events, seems to be moving into a channeling vortex from which there is no escape. Well-intentioned people see that modern nuclear warfare is a disastrous option for all of humanity. Science, while bringing mankind many benefits, has brought the possibility of worldwide control and mutual mass destruction in its wake.

Power and Authority through Peace

The Bible predicts that the Antichrist, the last world dictator, will gain power and authority through diplomatic and peacemaking efforts. Antiochus Epiphanies, the Syrian King (175-164 BC), who invaded Israel, went into the Holy Place and offered a pig upon the altar, a religious sacrilege for the Jews. Epiphanies (literally, "the shining one") is a type of the final Antichrist. The Bible states regarding Antiochus that "he shall come in peaceably and obtain the kingdom by flatteries . . . He shall work deceitfully . . . he shall enter peaceably."[2] The last great world dictator will also be a master of diplomacy and peacemaking efforts, possessing great oratorical powers of persuasion. Because of these abilities, as well as the desperate situation in the world, he will be given leadership willingly by other leaders of the world at the conference table.[3] Dangers such as rogue nations with nuclear weapons and terrorists will only cause the world to move to more autocratic control, involving more loss of freedom to the nations of the world and more power given to a charismatic leader.

—9—

A Holding Stage To The Next Great Event

The Rapture of the Church

The world is now in a holding stage until the next event on God's prophetic calendar. This event will be the "Rapture" which is the removal of the true church from this earth. There are no prophecies that need to be fulfilled before the Rapture. The Rapture will be followed by a series of events and prophecies that will culminate in the Day of the Lord. The Rapture is an imminent event and even the first generation of believers was looking for the return of Christ. Although the word "rapture" itself is not found in the Bible, the Latin term *rapere* meaning "to snatch up" is an adequate description of what is described in 1 Thessalonians 4:13-17:

> But I would not have you to be ignorant, brethren, concerning them which are asleep, that ye sorrow not, even as others which have no hope. For if we believe that Jesus died and rose again, even so them also which sleep in Jesus will God bring with him. For this we say unto you by the word of the Lord, that we which are alive and remain unto the coming of the Lord shall not prevent [precede]

them which are asleep. For the Lord himself shall descend from heaven with a shout, with the voice of the archangel, and with the trump of God: and the dead in Christ shall rise first: Then we which are alive and remain shall be caught up together with them in the clouds, to meet the Lord in the air: and so shall we ever be with the Lord.

Although the teaching of the Rapture may seem like a fantasy to some, especially since the sale of a prophetic fiction series including the book, *Left Behind*, it is as certain as the gospel of the death and resurrection of Christ.

For if we believe that Jesus died again and rose again, even so them also which sleep in Jesus will God bring with him (1 Thessalonians 4:14).

The Rapture was predicted by Christ when He described His coming again for His disciples for whom He was going to prepare a place.

Let not your heart be troubled: ye believe in God, believe also in me. In my Father's house are many mansions: if it were not so, I would have told you. I go to prepare a place for you. And if I go and prepare a place for you, I will come again, and receive you unto myself; that where I am, there ye may be also (John 14:1-3).

We are presently in the "mystery" program of God. A mystery in the New Testament is not something that is presently mysterious or unknown, but something that was not revealed to the believers in Old Testament times. These mysteries have been revealed to the church today. The present church age and the Rapture of the church are called "mysteries" in the

Bible, and the apostle Paul gave further disclosure of these mysteries.[1] The church is used in the universal sense instead of the local or denominational sense in Ephesians 3:10. The term "church" as used in this writing refers to all who have been saved beginning at the Day of Pentecost, from Acts chapter two, out of every race and denomination and it culminates with the Rapture of the church. The next event on God's clock is the Rapture of the church. As signs were given primarily to the Jewish nation,[2] to authenticate Jesus as the Messiah, there are no signs or prophetic events that need to be fulfilled before the Rapture.

The Rapture and the Day of the Lord

The Rapture is variously called the "Day of Christ" and the "Day of the Lord Jesus" or the "Day of the Lord Jesus Christ" in the New Testament and it precedes the "Day of the Lord."[3] In contrast to the Rapture, the "Day of the Lord" is that period of time which begins with the return of Christ with His church to earth to defeat the Antichrist and his armies, and includes the one thousand year reign of Christ over this present earth. First and Second Thessalonians are books that were written to clear up misconceptions regarding the coming of Christ. First Thessalonians presents the hope of the Rapture to comfort believers; who were expecting the return of Christ in their lifetime, since some of their loved ones had died and Christ had not returned. Paul indicated that the spiritual experience of those who died is in no way going to be inferior to those who are living at His return. In fact, the dead in Christ will rise first! First Thessalonians presents the comfort in an imminent Rapture and details the fact that the believer is rescued from the coming wrath upon the earth.[4] The coming of Christ at the Rapture is mentioned at the end of every chapter in 1 Thessalonians while practical Christian living instruction are given in light of this imminent hope.[5] Due to the persecution of the Thessalonian church, the early believers could have thought that they were in the time of tribulation, or at least close to the Day of the Lord.

Two Great Events before the Day of the Lord

Paul writes 2 Thessalonians to enumerate two great events that must occur on earth before the Day of the Lord.

> For the secret power of lawlessness is already at work; but the one who now holds it back will continue to do so till he is taken out of the way (2 Thessalonians 2:7 New International Version).

The Removal of the Hinderer

The first event will be the removal of the hinderer of lawlessness and iniquity. The final events, or signs in the book of Revelation cannot be completed until this hinderer of iniquity is removed. Although expositors today may have differences of opinion on who the hinderer of sin is, apparently the Thessalonian believers had been verbally taught about prophetic events and knew who this hinderer was.[6] An Old Testament passage that Jewish believers especially would know is Genesis 6:3:

> And the LORD said, My Spirit shall not always strive with man, for that he also is flesh: yet his days shall be an hundred and twenty years.

There would be a time when the Holy Spirit would stop restraining the wickedness of men, and judgment from God would inevitably follow. In the antediluvian age this meant that a worldwide flood would come upon the world to destroy mankind. However, the grace of God is evident even in this ancient time as Noah who "found grace in the eyes of the Lord" was selected to build an ark and obeyed God in doing so. This was a testimony to the world, and God gave men an opportunity to repent while the ark was being built.[7] Noah was "a preacher of righteousness" to that generation; protected in the ark and he and his family were saved from the flood. However, before Noah was instructed to build the ark, another witness to this wicked pre-flood generation was Enoch. It is said of Enoch that "he walked with God: and he was not; for God took him" (Genesis 5:24). Enoch was mysteriously translated from this earth never to see natural death. This is a historical example of a man who was caught up to heaven to be with God and could serve as a type of the translation of the church. Noah could also serve as a type of the nation of Israel being preserved through the Great Tribulation. The Holy Spirit is the restrainer of sin, but God designed to restrain sin basically through the intermediate agency of men. The men who restrained sin in this ancient age were godly men like Enoch and Noah. While Jesus was on earth, He predicted the coming and the work of the Holy Spirit through the church.

> And when he is come, he will reprove the world of sin, and of righteousness, and of judgment: of sin, because they believe not on me; of righteousness, because I go to my Father, and ye see me no more; of judgment, because the prince of this world is judged (John 16:8-11).

The Holy Spirit would convict the world through the agency of the Good News of the death and resurrection of Christ. It was at the cross where Satan, the prince of this world, was judged, and unbelief in Jesus the Savior and Messiah became the condemning sin of man. When Jesus left this earth, His disciples through the power of the Spirit would be that convicting and restraining force upon mankind.

It follows that the church's message of the gospel, by the power of the Holy Spirit, is the restraining force hindering sin in the world today. The church age is the age of the universal indwelling of the Spirit in believers. The church itself is called the "temple of the Spirit."

> In whom all the building fitly framed together groweth unto the holy temple in the Lord: . . . For an habitation of God through the Spirit (Ephesians 2:21-22b).

Regarding the hinderer, the Scriptures state: "until he be taken *out of the way*" which literally means the He is taken *out of the midst*. He is supernaturally removed from the midst of the people upon the earth. This describes the removal of the church from the midst of mankind at the end of the church age. The function of the Holy Spirit, after the Rapture, will resort back in similarity to His function in the Old Testament as the restrainer of sin through chosen individuals from the Jewish nation and as the agent of the new birth. The church as the entity, or temple of the Spirit, will no longer be the restraining force from sin in the Tribulation period nor will there be a universal dwelling of believers as there is now during the church age. This will permit, at the beginning of the Tribulation, the great delusion which will cause the world to accept the Antichrist.[8]

When the church is removed by the Rapture, the striving of the Spirit will temporarily cease among men, allowing the second great event which precedes the Day of the Lord to take place.

The Great Rebellion

> Do not let anyone deceive you in any way, for that day will not come until the rebellion occurs and the man of lawlessness is revealed…(2 Thessalonians 2:3a NIV).

The second event that occurs before the Day of the Lord will be the great rebellion, or departure from the truth which descends upon the world through the Antichrist. Although rebellion is with us today through the means of liberal religion, the final culmination of this rebellion is in the worship of one man:

> [The Antichrist] Who opposeth and exalteth himself above all that is called God, or that is worshipped; so that he as God sitteth in the temple of God, shewing himself that he is God (2 Thessalonians 2:4).

The Time of the Beginning of the Tribulation

The Tribulation period officially begins with the signing of the peace covenant with Israel. However, there may be a period of time, possibly at least a year, between the Rapture and the signing of the covenant for the Antichrist to consolidate his power. Temporarily, at the beginning of the Tribulation period, there will be no believers on earth providing insight to world events. There will be an eerie pseudo peace because evil has completely taken over the world, allowing the Antichrist to accomplish such apparent great feats as presiding over a temporary peace settlement in the Middle East and gaining worldwide leadership. The Rapture will be a mystery to the world. An explanation could be offered contending that this disappearance of people was a judgment of God removing people standing in the way of the world's evolutionary process to peace and unity. Furthermore, the number of believers could be greatly reduced at the Rapture because of worldwide religious apostasy, causing the Rapture to be a mysterious, but not earthshaking event.[9]

The Rapture and the Judgment Seat of Christ

While the Tribulation period is about to begin on earth, the judgment seat of Christ will occur in heaven. " . . . For we shall all stand before the judgment seat of Christ" (Romans 14:10b). This is the Bema seat where believers in Christ will receive reward for their service to Christ. It is pictured by a raised platform where a judge sat to give out awards at the Athenian games. Service to God rather than sin is the issue at the Bema Seat. This is a different judgment than the Great White Throne Judgment. There will be no examination to see whether the participant is in the "Book of Life" as only the saved will appear there.

The Basis of the Judgment

First of all, this judgment will be about faithfulness in service. "Moreover it is required in stewards, that a man be found faithful" (1 Corinthians 4:2).

Secondly, it will be according to the motives for serving the Lord in the church. The apostle Paul is clear that all wrong motives that are hidden from people in this life will be brought to light in that day.

> Therefore judge nothing before the time, until the Lord come, who both will bring to light the hidden things of darkness, and will make manifest the counsels of the hearts: and then shall every man have praise of God (1 Corinthians 4:5).

Some believers in Corinth were carnal because they had a party spirit demonstrated by the fact that they were praising the man rather than God. Any self-promotion or exaltation of a man indicates a wrong motive. The correct motives for service are exemplified by the apostle Paul.

The first correct motive is the genuine desire to serve to please God alone.

> So we make it our goal to please him, whether we are at home in the body or away from it (2 Corinthians 5:9 NIV).

The second correct motive is the genuine fear, or reverence of God because of the fact that believers will appear at the judgment seat of Christ.

> Knowing therefore the terror [fear] of the Lord, we persuade men (2 Corinthians 5:11).

The third correct motive is the great love Christ has for us which should inspire us to live for Him rather than ourselves.

> For the love of Christ constraineth us; because we thus judge, that if one died for all then were all dead: And that

he died for all, that they which live should not henceforth live unto themselves, but unto him which died for them, and rose again (2 Corinthians 5:14-15).

The Result of the Judgment

The result will be that all works done by incorrect motives will be burned. The believer will suffer loss of reward, but not loss of salvation.

Every man's work shall be made manifest: for the day shall declare it, because it shall be revealed by fire; and the fire shall try every man's work of what sort it is. If any man's work abide which he hath built thereupon, [the one foundation of Christ] he shall receive a reward. If any man's work shall be burned, he shall suffer loss: but he himself shall be saved; yet so as by fire (1 Corinthians. 3:13-15).

—10—

Will The Real Christ Please Stand Up?

"For there shall arise false Christs and false prophets."[1]

Back in the 1950s and 1960s during black and white television, Gary Moore hosted a show called "To Tell the Truth." Only one of the three contestants would be telling the truth as to his identity. Panel members would ask them questions and then guess which one was the real individual. Gary, at the conclusion would say "Will the real _____ please stand up?"

The Genuine Christ Came in the Name of His Father

Regarding believers in Christ, Scripture declares:

> . . . We are in him that is true [genuine], even in his Son Jesus Christ. This is the true God, and eternal life (I John 5:20b).

The stakes are high as eternal life depends on what is believed about Christ. Who is the genuine Christ? The Bible defines the difference between the false Christ and the genuine Christ.

> I am come in my Father's name, and ye receive me not; if
> another shall come in his own name, him ye will receive. How
> can ye believe, who receive honor one of another, and seek
> not the honor that cometh from God only? (John 5:43-44).

The genuine Christ came in the name of the Father and humbly submitted to His will and direction on earth while being an example to men on earth about humble submission to God. The false Christ will come in his own name while exalting himself. He will be received by many because men find his self-aggrandizement similar to their own. When men naturally seek their own glory and their own praise, they cannot at the same time truly believe on the genuine Christ. Actually, the genuine Christ vs. the false Christ illustrates the battle which rages within man. Do I live for myself to exalt self or do I live for God and obey Him?

The Uniqueness of the Christ

The characteristic of liberal religion is to deny the uniqueness of Christ. The Bible state that Jesus Christ is unique among men and has revealed the character of God the Father in human form. The incarnation of the Son of God is presented succinctly in these words by one who witnessed His works and heard His teachings upon the earth.

> And the Word was made flesh, and dwelt among us (and
> we beheld his glory, the glory of the only begotten of the
> Father,) full of grace and truth. . . . No man has seen God
> at any time; the only begotten Son, who is in the bosom of
> the Father, he hath declared Him (John 1:14, 18).

The words *only begotten* do not mean born, in the natural sense, but means Christ was *unique*. He has been the only One who has seen the full essence of God and can give full disclosure of God. When the Bible states that "He declared Him," it means that the early ministry of Christ exhibited what the Father was truly like. The Father Himself gives testimony to the fact that He is the unique Son of God and gave a little glimpse of His future glory at the Mount of Transfiguration. When Peter suggested they make three tabernacles honoring Jesus, Moses, and Elijah, thereby putting all three of these prophets on an equal level, God Himself rejected this idea of Peter by saying:

> . . . This is my beloved Son, in whom I am well pleased; hear ye him (Matthew 17:5b).

The testimony of John the Baptist, the works of Christ, the Father, and the Old Testament Scriptures all witness that Christ was the unique Son of God and therefore the genuine Christ.[2] There is exclusivity about the means of salvation and the path to God. This path is found in John 14:6:

> Jesus saith unto him, I am the way, the truth, and the life, no man cometh unto the Father, but by me.

Liberal Religion and the Illogical Source for the Genuine Christ

Liberal religion will seek to make Christ something less than He was by giving Him honor as a good teacher on par with other prophets such as Moses and even Muhammad. On religious holidays articles will be run in major news magazines talking about the quest for "the historical Jesus." It is argued that the Gospels, Matthew, Mark, Luke, and John are less than reliable historical documents and that modern scholarship must uncover the genuine Christ. This so called scholarly search impugns the witnesses of Christ in the first century and implies that the early disciples embellished the account of their Messiah.

However, it is illogical that here in the twenty-first century, living far away in time from the death and resurrection, one could better discover the real Christ than those who claimed to have seen Him in that first century. It seems to be arrogant that two millennia after the events we are better able to discover the genuine Christ. There is no middle ground regarding the genuine Christ. Either He is the Messiah as the New Testament documents contend, and we need to bow before Him or He is a liar or a lunatic who would disqualify Himself from even being a good human teacher or prophet. However, even religious liberals acknowledge the excellent teachings of Christ such as the Sermon on the Mount.

The Logical Evidence for the Genuine Christ is the Accuracy of the Written Documents

Because of the extraordinary claims of Christ, the accuracy of the written documents have been attacked. It is argued that because the Gospels were written later, sometime after Jesus walked the earth, the accounts about Him were embellished. It is contended that the idea of Jesus as the unique Son of God was invented by the church rather than revealed by God to the church. Conservative scholarship date the Gospel accounts from 50-60 AD and puts the Gospel of John at 85-90 AD. There was simply not enough time after the actual events for the accounts to be embellished. There were still enough believers living, who were close to the events, who would have known whether the events were embellished by the writers of the Gospels. Two of the Gospels, Matthew and John, were written by two of the early twelve disciples, who were with Jesus and followed Him in His ministry on earth. Another of the Gospels was written by Mark who was a disciple of the apostle Peter. Peter was one of the inner band of three along with James and the aforementioned apostle, John.

The Qualifications of the Writers

The Gospel of Luke was written by Luke who was a doctor, an early historian, and a companion of the apostle Paul on his missionary journeys. Luke used sources for his account since he was a second generation witness but claimed he ". . . had perfect understanding of all things from the very first . . ." (Luke 1:3). Luke also wrote the book of Acts; a historical account of the early Christian church. The accuracy of the Gospel of John is questioned because it was written later than the other three and is more theological than the others. However, who would be better able to give a theological discourse on the unique Son of God along with some of the historical events than: "the disciple whom Jesus loved." He was one of the inner band of three whom Jesus taught, along with His brother James and Peter. John was the disciple at the Cross when Jesus died and the one who went into the tomb with Peter after Jesus was raised.

The Resurrection Event was Well Known, but Still Denied

If the resurrection of Jesus was witnessed by one or just a few it might be passed off as a hallucination or wishful thinking. However it is detailed in Scripture that the resurrected Christ was witnessed by many.[3] Regarding the resurrection of Christ, Paul contended to King Agrippa that the events of the death and resurrection of Christ should be known even to this unbelieving monarch "for this thing was not done in a corner."[4] The reason that the Jews persecuted, and even killed believers in the early church was because of their proclamation that God had raised the one from the dead whom they had crucified. The message of the death and resurrection was well known in Jerusalem at that time and later went beyond Israel to the outer parts of the Roman Empire in Asia Minor. There were many believers in the Roman Empire by the time the Gospel accounts were written, and they knew that the Gospel writers' accounts were truly accurate.

The Disciples were Taught by Christ for 40 Days

Furthermore, Jesus taught the disciples for forty days after His resurrection allowing them to witness His resurrected body, hear Him teach, eat with Him, and even touch Him. The fact that Christ ate with them, and they could touch Him, proved this was more than a "spiritual" resurrection but rather involved a literal physical body.[5] The writer Luke contends that Jesus presented Himself alive after His suffering, ". . . by many infallible [convincing] proofs, appearing to them over a period of forty days and speaking of the things concerning the kingdom of God."[6] The disciples, Mary, and Thomas physically touched Him after His resurrection.[7] There is a preponderance of historical evidence concerning the resurrection of Christ. The gospel is rooted in facts that actually happened in history and is therefore as real as the fact that George Washington lived in America.

The Jews Failure to Refute the Resurrection

To refute the disciples' message of the resurrection of Christ the Jews could have gone to the tomb to produce the dead body. Because they could not, they were reduced to the lie that the disciples had stolen the body and to the action of attempting to stifle the message through persecution. The story that the disciples stole the body does not face the fact that the disciples were unbelieving, spiritually defeated, and cowering in fear after the crucifixion of Christ. They were in no mood for such a brazen attempt at thievery! The tomb had been sealed with a large stone and guarded by soldiers to prevent that possibility.[8]

The Evidence of the Changed Life of the Depressed Apostles

Not only is there evidence of the empty tomb, but also there is evidence of the changed life of the early disciples. They went from a cowering fearful, defeated, and a depressed group hiding in the upper room in fear of the Jews to those who boldly proclaimed the resurrection of Christ to the Jews in Jerusalem in the face of much opposition and persecution.

The Evidence of the Enduring Christian Faith

The existence, spread, and growth of Christianity to the twenty-first century, despite continued persecution and resistance down through history indicates the truth and power of that message.

The Promise of the Genuine Christ

The genuine Christ has given a promise to all men who would trust in Him alone for salvation apart from religious deeds and effort.

And this is the promise that he hath promised us, even eternal life (I John 2:25).

This is not only an eternal life of duration, but also a new quality of life. Jesus said:

The thief cometh not, but to steal, and to kill, and to destroy: I am come that they might have life, and that they might have it more abundantly (John 10:10).

Whereas Satan destroys through physical death and a type of life that brings shame, depression, and disappointment, Jesus offers a life of rest which brings love, peace, and joy. He Himself is that life in which the believer participates when He receives Christ.[9] The believer is vitally linked in union to Christ when he believes, participating in the very life of Christ Himself and therefore has an inherent power to live like Christ.

The Genuine Christ as the Object Lesson of the Spirit and Power

Jesus the Trailblazer

Jesus Himself was the perfect pattern and object lesson for a life lived in the power of the Spirit. He was the pioneer, or trailblazer for all mankind to illustrate a life of dependence upon and submission to the Father.[10]

The Need to be "Born Again"

Although all men are made in the image of God which is the basis for a measure of human goodness, man must be "born again" of the Spirit through faith in Christ to be able to be completely restored unto that image. Man in his natural state is able to do some apparent "good" things in the sight of other men which are really energized by the flesh rather than by the Spirit. In fact, the "good deeds" attained by the natural man may look very similar to the deeds realized by the man who is genuinely saved. The difference lies in the source and motivation of a life. A life will either be energized by living to glorify self, hoping to be accepted by what is accomplished, or it will be energized by the Holy Spirit, seeking glory for Christ in obedience to Him. This would be because of the work of Christ accomplished for our salvation upon the cross. Jesus began his ministry "being full of the Holy Spirit,"[11] and was continually energized by submission to the Father and the power of the Spirit.

The Genuine New Age

The Beginning of the Last Days

This present church age is the age of the universal indwelling of the Holy Spirit, but it pales in comparison to the millennial age to come when the power of Christ shall be evident to all mankind. This present church age is said to be the beginning of the Last Days which will usher in the kingdom of God and Christ upon the present earth.[1]

God's Further Design for this Present Earth

We can be assured that this earth will be spared from a nuclear annihilation by the truth that God has further design for this present earth. That design, or plan is for Jesus Christ to rule on this earth for one thousand years as a benevolent King. However, this can only be accomplished by defeating those who would bring mutual destruction to this earth. The Bible speaks of the fact that one of the purposes of God in the future is to "destroy them who destroy the earth" (Revelation 11:18). No matter how unflattering it might seem, man left to his own self-interest and desire for power would mutually self-destruct. Two world wars and the horrors and ravages by brutal dictators show the destruction that mankind can bring upon himself and to the earth through the godless philosophies which bring statism.

Nuclear Warfare in the Tribulation Period

Although apparent nuclear disarmament has taken place, nations may secretly hide nuclear stockpiles. It is unlikely that the world would possess nuclear weapons and never use them in the future. In fact, it seems that nuclear warfare may take place when Magog (Russia) invades Israel.[2] The writers of Scripture could only describe nuclear warfare in terminology they were familiar. Such terms as overflowing rain and fire and brimstone could possibly be referring to nuclear warfare.[3]

Birth Pangs Leading to the Genuine New Age

The imagery of a woman giving birth is used by the Bible to illustrate that the Rapture will be followed by swift destruction after the rise of Antichrist and the outpouring of the wrath of God upon the earth.

> For when they shall say, Peace and safety; then sudden destruction cometh upon them, as travail upon a woman with child; and they shall not escape (1 Thessalonians 5:3).

The Appearance of False Christs, with World Wars and Natural Devastations

This church age will be characterized by the appearance of false Christs, world wars (nation against nation and kingdom against kingdom), and natural devastations such as famines and earthquakes.[4] These events will also characterize the first half of the Tribulation. The "new age" will follow the birth pangs of the second half of Tribulation period which is called the Great Tribulation because of the severity of its judgments. The seven years of tribulation upon the earth is the intermediate period between the Rapture and the second coming of Christ before He sets up His millennial reign.

The Entrants to the Real New Age

Despite the severity of the Great Tribulation period, there will be those who physically survive and will face the judgment of the nations.

> For then shall be the great tribulation, such as was not since the beginning of the world to this time, no, nor ever shall be. And except those days should be shortened, there should no flesh be saved: but for the elect's sake those days shall be shortened (Matthew 24:21-22).

Then those who believe will enter into the new age of the Millennium.

Matthew 24:27-44 is talking about the aspect of the second coming of the Lord, at the end of the Tribulation, rather than the Rapture of the church which occurs before the Tribulation.

> Then shall two be in the field; the one shall be taken, and the other left, two women shall be grinding at the mill; the one shall be taken, and the other left (Matthew 24:40-41).

Those who are left are believers who will enter into the Millennium after the judgment of the nations. The remainder of humanity will be taken into judgment by Christ at the judgment of the nations. A great number of people will be saved during the Tribulation period but many of them will become martyrs for their faith.[5] People that have heard the gospel before the Rapture will likely come under the strong delusion of the lie of the Antichrist and lose their opportunity. Speaking of the Antichrist, Scripture states:

> Even him, whose coming is after the working of Satan with all power and signs and lying wonders, and with all deceivableness of unrighteousness in them that perish; because they received not the love of the truth, that they might be saved (2 Thessalonians 2:9-10).

A Believing Remnant of Israel

There will be a believing remnant of Israel, supernaturally protected by God that will enter into the new age of the millennium. This is what the apostle Paul predicted when he stated:

> And so all Israel shall be saved: as it is written, There shall come out of Sion, the Deliverer, and shall turn away ungodliness from Jacob (Romans 11:26).

In the middle of the Tribulation the Antichrist will break his covenant of protection for Israel and declare himself to be God.

> Who opposeth and exalteth himself above all that is called God, or that is worshipped; so that he as God sitteth in the temple of God, shewing himself that is God (2 Thessalonians 2:4).

Many of the Jewish nation will be converted to Christ at the defeat of Magog (Russia) and therefore, will reject the demand of the Antichrist to be worshipped.

> So the house of Israel shall know that I am the Lord their God from that day and forward (Ezekiel 39:22).

This will begin the worst period of anti-Semitism in history with an unparalleled persecution of the Jewish people. Revelation chapter 12 speaks, in figurative language, of the protection that God will give Israel during this time. The dragon and the serpent represent Satan, the woman is Israel, and the flood is the armies sent out by Satan.

First of all, God will provide a place of protection for Israel in an unspecified place in the wilderness for the last three and a half years of the Tribulation.

> And to the woman were given two wings of a great eagle, that she might fly into the wilderness, into her place, where she is nourished for a time and times, and half a time, [3 ½ years] from the face of the serpent (Revelation 12:14).

Secondly, an earthquake is sent by God to swallow up the armies that were sent to pursue Israel.

> And the earth helped the woman, and the earth opened her mouth, and swallowed up the flood which the dragon cast out of his mouth (Revelation 12:16).

The Judgment of the Nations

> When the Son of man shall come in his glory, and all his holy angels with him, then shall he sit upon the throne of

his glory: And before him shall be gathered all nations; and he shall separate them one from another, as a shepherd divideth the sheep from the goats; And he shall set the sheep on his right hand, but the goats on the left. Then shall the king say unto them on his right hand, Come, ye blessed of my Father, inherit the kingdom prepared for you from the foundation of the world (Matthew 25:31-34).

The basis of the judgment

The basis of this judgment is how the nations treated the persecuted Jews during the Tribulation. As salvation has always been by grace through faith, they have demonstrated their faith by their help for the Jewish people during this terrible period of anti-Semitism. As the church has already been raptured, the "brethren" of Christ are the Jewish people:

For I was an hungred, and ye gave me meat: I was thirsty, and ye gave me drink: I was a stranger, and ye took me in: Naked, and ye clothed me: I was sick, and ye visited me: I was in prison, and ye came unto me. Then shall the righteous answer him, saying, Lord, when saw we thee an hungred, and fed thee? or thirsty, and gave thee drink? When saw we thee a stranger, and took thee in? or naked, and clothed thee? Or when saw we thee sick, or in prison, and came unto thee? And the King shall answer and say unto them, Verily I say unto you, Inasmuch as ye have done it unto the one of the least of these my brethren, ye have done it unto me (Matthew 25:35-40).

The result of the judgment

The sheep, who are believing Gentiles, have physically survived the Tribulation period and will enter into the

Millennium in their mortal bodies. The goats are unbelieving Gentiles who are taken away in judgment.

> Then shall he say also unto them on the left hand, depart from me ye cursed, into everlasting fire, prepared for the devil and his angels (Matthew 25:41).

The Characteristics of the Genuine New Age

The world is now moving forward to a real new age ushered in by Jesus Christ Himself. It will be a thousand years of an unparalleled time of peace and prosperity that only Christ Himself could bring. Believers in Christ will rule with Him. Satan will be bound; justice and the full knowledge of God will prevail upon this present earth.[6] What man failed to gain by the efforts of the last great world dictator through autocratic government, the Messiah will institute through a benevolent rulership of one thousand years.

A Time of Universal Indwelling and Filling of the Spirit

This will be a time predicted by the prophet Joel which will be characterized by the fullness, or universal indwelling, and filling of the Holy Spirit in both Jewish and Gentile believers in Christ.

> And it shall come to pass afterward that I will pour out my spirit upon all flesh . . . (Joel 2:28a).

The filling of the Sprit will be much more on display than it is among the believers today in the church age.

A Time when the Curse of Sickness and Death is Minimized

The curse of sin with its result of sickness and death will be largely removed. However, there will be physical death as a penal measure in dealing with overt rebellion against Christ.

> There shall be no more thence and infant of days, nor an old man that hath not filled his days: for the child shall die a hundred years old, but the sinner being a hundred years old shall be accursed (Isaiah 65:20).

Physical death will ultimately and finally be eliminated after the one thousand year rule of Christ and therefore will be the "last enemy" to be destroyed before the eternal state.

A Time of Longevity of Life and Freedom from Oppression

There will be longevity of life and freedom from oppression.[7] There will be no brutal dictators or wicked leaders who will oppress mankind.

> They shall not hurt nor destroy in all my holy mountain . . . (Isaiah 11:9a).

A Time of a Perfect Economic System

Economic problems will be solved as there will be a perfect economic system which may include a fully developed industrialized society, including agriculture and manufacturing, which will bring unparalleled economic growth and prosperity.

And they shall build houses and inhabit them, and they shall plant vineyards and eat the fruit of them (Isaiah 65:21).

A Time of a Unified Worship and World Government

There will be a unified worship of God and a unified godly world government. " . . . That unto me every knee shall bow, and every tongue shall swear" (Isaiah 45:23b). The unity that man sought and coveted upon earth will finally arrive in the person of Christ. The government will deal with any open rebellion and disobedience, and doing the will of God will be facilitated because of the filling of the Spirit, the binding of Satan, and the elimination of the world system which is controlled by Satan.[8] In the Millennium, temptation can only come from the sinful nature of man.[9]

A Time of an Involvement of Present Day Church Believers in the Millennial Age

This millennial hope also relates to the church today. Although our destiny is the heavenly Jerusalem, we will reign from the New Jerusalem on the earth. The Bible predicts:

And saviors shall come up on mount Zion to judge the mount of Esau; and the kingdom shall be the LORD's (Obadiah 21).

Those who are part of the "resurrection of life" will be priests who will rule with Christ:

Blessed and holy is he that hath part in the first resurrection: on such the second death hath no power, but they shall be priests of God and of Christ, and shall reign with him a thousand years (Revelation 20:6).

Final Events For Mankind

The Cross of Christ has a cosmic effect that not only involves the redemption of individual man, but also has potentially purchased the reconciliation of the whole world to God. The book of Revelation sets that scene of the final reconciliation process.[1]

The Bible indicates that there will be a time when there can no longer be a change in the moral state of man:

> He that is unjust, let him be unjust still: and he which is filthy, let him be filthy still: and he that is righteous, let him be righteous still: and he that is holy, let him be holy still (Revelation 22:11).

The Bible indicates that the time for change is in this present life:

> And as it is appointed unto men once to die, but after this the judgment (Hebrews 9:27).

The Final Test

The Scriptures indicate that Satan will be loosed from the Abyss after the one thousand years and will lead an insurrection of men against Christ, who will in turn assault the capital city of Jerusalem. This rebellion is quickly quashed by the fire of God.[2] The question remains: Why would Satan be let out of prison after a thousand years? God seems to be illustrating, by this final test of man, that even a perfect environment for man is not the final solution. The problem exists in the sinful, rebellious hearts of men. People will be born with fallen sin natures during these one thousand years, and they will inwardly chafe at the rule of Christ. When Satan leads a rebellion, they will eagerly follow him. Such forms of government as socialism, statism, communism, democracy, and even a perfect benevolent dictatorship bringing a perfect environment cannot bring a complete utopia to man. His inner being, or heart must be changed by God Himself through Christ.

Democracy seems to be the best form of government in this present age because of man's sin nature. America's democracy has been a republic based on Judeo-Christian laws and values, which give man the ability to govern himself. In the end result, only Christ can give the individual, as he "walks in the Spirit," the ability of self-government.

Events that will Eliminate the Curse of Sin

Events that will occur after the millennial reign of Christ will eliminate everything that is affected by the curse of sin upon the planet. Physical death is an enemy of God and man, this will be eliminated after the one thousand year rule of Christ on earth. The apostle Paul speaks about this future rule of God the Father:

> Then cometh the end, when he [Christ] shall have delivered up
> the kingdom to God, even the Father; when he shall have put

down all rule and all authority and power. For he must reign, till he hath put all enemies under his feet. The last enemy that shall be destroyed is death (1 Corinthians 15:24-26).

The Great White Throne Judgment

The Great White Throne Judgment follows the final insurrection led by Satan and it occurs after the Millennium. The participants of this judgment are the spiritually dead who have rejected Christ, as this is the final judgment.

> And I saw a great white throne, and him that sat on it, from whose face the earth and heaven fled away; and there was found no place for them. And I saw the dead, small and great, stand before God; and the books were opened: and another book was opened, which is the book of life: and the dead were judged out of those things which were written in the books, according to their works. And the sea gave up the dead which were in it; and death and hell delivered up the dead which were in them: and they were judged every man according to their works. And death and hell were cast into the lake of fire. This is the second death. And whosoever was not found written in the book of life was cast into the lake of fire (Revelation 20:11-15).

The basis of the Great White Throne Judgment rests on three things:

1. The judgment rests on whether or not the names of these individuals were written in the Book of Life. This Book of Life was opened "And whosoever was not found written in the book of life was cast into the lake of fire" (Revelation 20:15).

The Lord knows His own, and His people will demonstrate a life that is not characterized by iniquity. This agrees with the truth of Scripture. No one who continues to sin has either seen him or known him (I John 3:6 NIV).

2.   The judgment is based on the Bible (a collection of books). They are judged according to the books as seen in Revelation 20:12:

And I saw the dead, small and great, stand before God; and the books were opened: and another book was opened, which is the book of life: and the dead were judged out of those things which were written in the books, according to their works.

Nevertheless the foundation of God standeth sure, having this seal, The Lord knoweth them that are his. And, Let everyone that nameth the name of Christ depart from iniquity (2 Timothy 2:19).

3.   This judgment is ". . . according to their works" (Revelation 20:12). Their works did not measure up because ". . . all have sinned and come short of the glory of God" (Romans 3:23). God is infinitely fair in judgment as ". . . he shall reward every man according to his works" (Matthew 16:27b). There will be degrees of judgment according to one's knowledge of the will of God. "But he that knew not, and did commit things worthy of stripes, shall be beaten with few stripes . . ." (Luke 12:48a).

The final destiny of the wicked, including those who rebelled against God with Satan after the Millennium, will be the lake of fire. Hades, or hell and the grave is a temporary place of torment, and it will deliver up all the lost to be cast into the lake of fire as a final point of destination. This is called the "second death" in Scripture.[3] Before this happens Satan will be relegated to the lake of fire where the Beast (the Antichrist) and the False Prophet have already been cast alive at the second coming of Christ.[4]

The Passing Away of the Present Heavens and Earth

The third event that will occur after the Millennium is the passing away of the present heaven and earth. The apostle Peter predicts:

> But the day of the Lord will come as a thief in the night, in the which the heavens shall pass away with a great noise, and the elements shall melt with fervent heat, the earth also, and the works that are therein shall be burned up (2 Peter 3:10).

Since both the atmospheric heavens and the earth have been contaminated by Satan, (the prince of the power of the air) a new pristine heaven and earth is necessary.[5]

The Arrival of the New Heaven and Earth

The fourth event, leading to the final eternal state, is the arrival of the new heaven and new earth. The apostle John records the arrival of this new heaven and earth:

> And I saw a new heaven and a new earth; for the first heaven and the first earth were passed away, and there was no more sea (Revelation 21:1).

The Descent of the Heavenly City

The last event recorded by John in the book of Revelation is the descent of the Holy City, the heavenly Jerusalem, which Christ has prepared for His people:

> And I John, saw the holy city, the new Jerusalem, coming down from God out of heaven, prepared as a bride adorned for her husband (Revelation 21:2).

The Inhabitants of the Heavenly City

The inhabitants of the heavenly city are depicted in Hebrews 12:22-23:

> But ye are come unto Mount Sion, and to the living God, the heavenly Jerusalem, and to an innumerable company of angels, to the general assembly and church of the first born, which are written in heaven, and to God the judge of all, and to the spirits of just men made perfect.

The most glorious inhabitant is the living God, accompanied by a countless group of angels. The New Jerusalem is where the people of God will dwell eternally. Included are those who have believed in Old Testament times, those who have believed in the church age, and those believers who died in the Tribulation period both Jew and Gentile.[6] Those who died in the church age will be resurrected at the Rapture before the Tribulation. Old Testament believers and tribulation believers will be resurrected after the Tribulation at the second coming of Christ. The Scriptures speak of resurrections that will occur after the Tribulation.

And at that time shall Michael stand up, the great prince which standeth for the children of thy people: and there shall be a time of trouble, such as never was since there was a nation even to that same time: and at that time thy people shall be delivered, every one that shall be found written in the book. Any many of them that sleep in the dust of the earth shall awake, Some to everlasting life, and some to shame and everlasting contempt (Daniel 12:1-2).

The Scriptures indicate that the Old Testament believers and the church have the common destination of the heavenly city.

- Regarding the Old Testament believers:

But now they desire a better country, that is, an heavenly: Wherefore God is not ashamed to be called their God: For he hath prepared for them a city (Hebrews 11:16).

- Regarding the church today:

God having provided some better thing for us, that they [the Old Testament believers] without us should not be made perfect (Hebrews 11:40).

Our hope, along with Old Testament believers who have died, is the heavenly hope of the New Jerusalem.

The Occupation of the Inhabitants of the Heavenly City

It is going to take the ages to come for us to learn the true extent of the riches of the grace and kindness to us through Christ.

That in the ages to come He might shew the exceeding riches of His grace in his kindness toward us through Christ Jesus (Ephesians 2:7).

Therefore, believers will be ever learning about God's grace and worshipping Him. Life in the New Jerusalem is beyond our present full understanding. However we are given glimpses of it in the Word of God.

- It is going to be a life of full fellowship with God.

It will be a different kind of knowledge of Him. The apostle John speaks of a new likeness to Christ and new knowledge of Christ.

Beloved now are we the sons of God, and it doth not yet appear what we shall be; but we know that, when he shall appear we will be like him: for we shall see him as he is (I John 3:2).

This knowledge will be "face to face" knowledge. It will be a giant step in spiritual knowledge, superseding our present knowledge of God through the written revelation of the Bible.

For now we see through a glass, darkly; but then face to face: now I know in part; but then I shall know even as also I am known (1 Corinthians 13:12).

- It will be a life of rest from conflict.

Blessed are the dead which die in the Lord from henceforth: Yea, saith the Spirit, that they may rest from their labors, and their works do follow them (Revelation 14:13).

Just think of a life of no more conflict with the sin nature and Satan and his world system.

- It will be a life full of joy and happiness.

And God shall wipe away all tears from their eyes; and there shall be no more death, neither sorrow, nor crying, neither shall there be any more pain: for the former things are passed away (Revelation 21:4).

There will be no more painful goodbyes by the separation of death. There will be no more pain through illness, disease, and emotional pain through fractured relationships here on earth among family members.

- It will be a life of rulership over this present earth with Christ.

The beatitude that teaches that the meek shall inherit the earth will be literally fulfilled.[7] The twenty-four elders in Revelation represent redeemed people.[8] More specifically Dwight Pentecost contends that the twenty-four elders are representative of the church when he states:[9]

Since, according to Revelation 5:8, these twenty-four elders are associated in a priestly act, which is never said of angels, they must be believer-priests associated with the Great High Priest.

These believer-priests will rule on this present earth. "And hast made us unto our God kings and priests: and we shall reign on the earth."[10] Hints are given in Scripture of this future rulership. The apostles are told they will judge the Twelve Tribes of Israel during the Millennium.

> And Jesus said unto them, verily I say unto you, that ye who have followed me, in the regeneration [millennium] when the Son of man shall sit on the throne of his glory, ye shall also sit upon the twelve thrones, judging the twelve tribes of Israel (Matthew 19:28).

The Bible speaks of the servants of God given rulership over cities.[11] The church believers, in their glorified bodies, will rule over people on this present earth who are in their earthly bodies. Christ already demonstrated, after His resurrection, that association between glorified beings with non-glorified beings was possible.

- It will be a life of worship and praise.

Finally, as great as a life of "face to face" knowledge of God possessing full happiness and joy and rulership with Christ is, the inhabitants of the heavenly city will be more occupied with the worship and praise of God than their experience of happiness and rulership with Christ. Along with the angels, the human inhabitants of the New Jerusalem will be forever occupied with the worship and praise of God for redemption.

> And they sung a new song, saying, Thou art worthy to take the book, and to open the seals thereof: for thou wast slain, and redeemed us to God by thy blood out of every kindred and tongue, and people, and nation (Revelation 5:9).

A Second Descent of the Heavenly City

> And I John saw the holy city, new Jerusalem, coming down
> from God out of heaven, prepared as a bride adorned for
> her husband (Revelation 21:2).

> And he carried me away in the spirit to a great and high
> mountain, and shewed me that great city, the holy Jerusalem,
> descending out of heaven from God (Revelation 21:10).

Prophetic scholar J. Dwight Pentecost contends:

> There are two descents of the city in [Revelation] chapter
> 21, one at the beginning of the Millennium, and the other
> at the commencement of the eternal state. The second
> verse in that chapter gives us its descent when the eternal
> state is come, and the tenth verse its descent for the
> Millennium.[12]

The first descent would be before the Millennium as
the city hovers over the present heavens and earth when the
present day church rules with Christ. However when the
present heavens and earth are destroyed, the heavenly city
will ascend back up to heaven. Then, after the creation of the
new heaven and new earth the Holy City will descend again to
hover over the heaven and earth. This glorious city is a cube
144,000 miles square with plenty of room for the redeemed of
all ages to inhabit. There is no temple as God the Father and
Jesus the Lamb, are the temple.[13] It needs no luminaries as the
glory of God will illumine it.[14] The gates will not be shut as
there is no night or darkness there.[15] The nations of the world
shall offer tribute to its glory.[16]

—13—

The Panorama Of The Ages

God's program for man is divided into a succession of ages (dispensations) in which he is tested as to whether he will be obedient to the revelation of responsibilities which God has given him.

First of all, these ages are progressive until they develop into a fuller "face to face" disclosure of God in the future eternal state. Today, in the church age, we live in the Last Days when there has been disclosure of God's son, Jesus Christ, by means of the revelation of Him through the Scriptures contained in the Old and New Testaments.

> God, who at sundry times and I in divers manners spake
> in time past unto the fathers by the prophets, hath in these
> last days spoken to us by his son . . . (Hebrews 1:1-2a).

This passage indicates that the revelation of God was piecemeal in the Old Testament as it was given by word of mouth, visions, dictation, and other means to God's appointed prophets. Before there was written revelation from God, the accounts of Creation and the Flood were passed down by tradition and word of mouth from generation to generation. Moses was the giver of the old covenant of the law to Israel which set down the requirements of a Holy God for his people.

The Old Testament emphasizes the uniqueness and Holiness of God. "Hear O Israel: The LORD our God is one LORD" (Deuteronomy 6:4). This verse does not deny the Trinity but emphasizes the uniqueness of God in that He is the only true God and that there is no one else like Him as opposed to the false gods, or idols of other nations. The oft repeated phrase in the Old Testament is "I am the LORD, there is none else." The two main names for God in the Old Testament, Jehovah and Elohim represent His veracity as a covenant keeping God along with His action as the powerful Creator. The Israelites illustrated, by their inability to keep the holy requirements of a great God, that a Saviour was needed to provide forgiveness for man. "For all have sinned and come short of the glory of God" (Romans 3:23). Although there is an emphasis on the holy requirements of God in the Old Testament, contrary to some liberal teaching, the God of the Old Testament is not different from the God of the New Testament. He is the same God who always keeps His Word and illustrates His compassion and mercy to those who love Him.

> Know therefore that the LORD thy God, he is God, the faithful God, which keepeth covenant and mercy with them that love and obey him and keep His commandments to a thousand generations (Deuteronomy 7:9).

The final disclosure of the grace and truth of God for this church age is in the person of Jesus Christ. The apostle John makes a differentiation between the age of the law and the church age when he states:

> For the law was given by Moses, but grace and truth came by Jesus Christ. No man hath seen God at any time; the

only begotten Son which is in the bosom of the Father, he hath declared him (John 1:17-18).

The disclosure of the unseen God in this church age came in the bodily form of Jesus, the Son, as He walked among us and fully explained by His life the requirements of the kingdom of God. He ultimately died to make a payment for the sins of mankind. He was the *only begotten, unique* Son of God, as His Father is the unique and only God. With the arrival of Christ to this earth darkness was lifted and new light was shown to mankind. ". . . The darkness is past and the true light now shineth" (I John 2:8b). The apostle Peter warns us to take heed to the revelation of the Word of God.

> We have also a more sure word of prophecy; whereunto ye do well that ye take heed, as unto a light that shineth in a dark place, until the day dawn and the day star arise in your hearts: Knowing this first, that no prophecy of the scripture is of any private interpretation. For the prophecy of scripture came not in old time by the will of man: but holy men of God spake as they were moved by the Holy Ghost (2 Peter 1:19-21).

The Scripture is the more sure Word of prophecy. In contrast to a future glimpse of the coming kingdom to Peter, James, and John on the Mount of Transfiguration, Scripture is the testimony of a multitude of many witnesses who saw Christ while He was on earth. God has no further revelation for this church age other than the Scriptures. Peter warns us to take heed unto this revelation until Christ returns. It is similar to the warning to the Hebrew believers:

Therefore we ought to give the more earnest heed to the things which we have heard, lest at any time we should let them slip (Hebrews 2:1).

The idea of the word *slip* is to *drift away* from the harbor as a ship not properly anchored. God has no other revelation for us in this age so we need to pay earnest attention to it through trusting obedience.

Secondly, although the revelation of God is progressive, the salvation of God is always by grace based on the death of Christ on the cross and His resurrection from the dead. Paul ties the Old Testament economy together with the New Testament when he states:

> Being justified freely by his grace through the redemption which is in Christ Jesus: Whom God has set forth to be a propitiation through faith in his blood, to declare his righteousness for the remission of sins that are past, through the forbearance of God, To declare, I say, at this time his righteousness: that he might be just, and the justifier of him which believeth in Jesus (Romans 3:24-26).

The atonement of the animal sacrifices for sin in the past Old Testament economy only illustrated the forbearance (patience) of God looking forward to the ultimate redeeming sacrifice of Christ. The Old Testament animal sacrifices for sin could never actually take away sin, but pictured the final one sacrifice of Christ, that would finally take away sin.

> And every priest standing daily ministering and offering oftentimes the same sacrifices, which can never take away sins: But this man, after he had offered one sacrifice for sins for ever, sat down at the right hand of God (Hebrews 10:11-12).

In this sense the Old Testament prepared us for the New Testament by illustrating that sin demanded the punishment of death because man failed to live up to the just law of God. It also illustrated that nothing less than the grace of God could triumph over sin. In the panorama of the ages, the sin and rebellion of man did not catch God by surprise and frustrate His plan. The backdrop of sin highlights the grace of God by magnifying His righteousness. Man's failure down through the ages is met by the grace of God.

> Moreover the law entered that the offense might abound. But where sin abounded, grace did much more abound (Romans 5:20).

The Age of Innocence and the Fall

In the age of innocence Adam and Eve were tested to see whether they would willingly obey one simple command of God. Notice the benevolence of God in providing access to every tree of the Garden of Eden except one:

> And the LORD God commanded the man, saying, Of every tree of the garden thou mayest freely eat (Genesis 2:16).

God did not create man to be a little automaton. He wanted a willing servant. Man was created in a state of innocence and unconfirmed holiness. God gave him a simple test to determine whether he would willingly obey Him:

> But of the tree of the knowledge of good and evil, thou shalt not eat of it: for in the day that thou eatest thou shalt surely die (Genesis 2:17).

Not only did the serpent deny the truth of the Word of God, he also cast aspersions on the goodness of God by indicating that God was withholding sovereignty from Adam and Eve. He declared:

> For God doth know that in the day ye eat thereof, then your eyes shall be opened, *and ye shall be as gods knowing good and evil* (Genesis 3:5). (Emphasis added by author.)

God created man that he might be satisfied with God Himself and His will for his life. The tempter instilled dissatisfaction within Adam and Eve regarding the goodness of God and His will. There was partial truth in the statement of the serpent. Adam and Eve did discover the difference between good and evil when they ate of the tree. Good is choosing to obey God, but they entered into this knowledge by disobedience. Now they were in the position where they habitually chose the evil and needed the clothing of redemption. This began an inherent suspicion and mistrust of the truth of what God has said in His Word which was passed on to all of us. It also began an era when man's conscience would fail him, and he would not live up to even what his conscience would tell him was the truth. Instead of being satisfied with God and submissive to His sovereignty, although he is a dependent and a mortal creature, man now struck out on his own as the prodigal. The way man has been tempted through the ages originated in the distant past in the Garden of Eden.

> And when the woman saw that the tree was good for food, and that it was pleasant to the eyes, and a tree to be desired to make one wise, she took of the fruit thereof, and did eat, and gave also unto her husband with her; and he did eat (Genesis 3:6).

There is a similarity in the avenues of temptation to the believer today which is through the world system (the cosmos).

> For all that is in the world, the lust of the flesh, and the lust of the eyes, and the pride of life, is not of the Father but is of the world (1 John 2:16).

The serpent tempted Eve with a fruit that was pleasant to the eyes (lust of the eyes), was good for food (lust of the flesh, or bodily appetites), and a tree desired to make one wise (the pride of life, literally the boasting of one's possessions or attainments). This is the way man has sought his independence from God down through the ages. It is serving and loving the gifts that God has given in His creation rather than serving and loving the Creator. The indictment of God against mankind is simply the idolatry of worshipping the creation instead of the Creator:

> Who changed the truth of God into a lie, and worshipped and served the creature more than the Creator, who is blessed forever. Amen (Romans 1:25).

The lesson, which we must constantly learn, is to keep our satisfaction and expectations in God Himself instead of anything this world system might have to offer. Our tendency, especially in the difficulties of life which cause distress and possibly depression, is to demand relief rather than to be seeking to develop a deeper relationship and knowledge of God. The teaching under the dispensation of the age of the law is the same as in the church age. The believer in Christ must be satisfied with progressively knowing and loving God, obeying Him out of a sense of trust rather than a slavish duty to gain acceptance from God.

That thou mayest love the LORD thy God, and that
thou mayest obey his voice, and that thou mayest cleave
unto him: *for he is thy life* and the length of thy days . . .
(Deuteronomy 30:20a). (Emphasis added by author.)

The apostle Paul captures it well when he states: "For
me to live is Christ" . . . and, "That I may know him and the
power of His resurrection."[1] He is the very source of spiritual
life including the abundant wellspring of life that God, as
the loving shepherd of our soul, who, wants to lavish on His
people.

> The thief cometh not, but to steal, and to kill, and to
> destroy: I am come that they might have life, and that they
> might have it more abundantly have it more abundantly
> (John 10:10).

> When Christ, *who is our life*, [Italics mine], shall appear, then
> shall ye also appear with Him in glory (Colossians 3:4).

A cursory look at the panorama of the ages will show
that man continually seeks to make life work through pride
in his attainments and sensual indulgence in the gifts of the
Creator rather than being satisfied with knowing and loving
the Creator. The gifts of God in creation are wonderful and to
be enjoyed with thanksgiving. True spirituality does not mean
we become ascetics or monks. In a context about material
possessions, Jesus gave us the formula for enjoying the material
gifts of God. It is to keep them in right perspective by putting
a quest of His kingdom and righteousness first: "But seek ye
first the kingdom of God, and his righteousness and all these
things shall be added unto you" (Matthew 6:33).

The Age of Conscience

The age of conscience began after the sin of Adam and Eve. They immediately showed a guilty conscience which involved hiding from God in cringing fear. They also sought to pacify their guilty conscience by clothing their nakedness before a Holy God.

> And they heard the voice of the LORD God walking in the garden during the cool of the day: and Adam and his wife hid themselves from the presence of the LORD God amongst the trees of the garden. And the LORD God called unto Adam, and said unto him, Where art thou? And he said, I heard thy voice in the garden, and I was afraid, because I was naked; and I hid myself. And he said, who told thee that thou wast naked? Hast thou eaten of the tree, whereof I commanded thee that thou shouldest not eat? (Genesis 3:8-11).

The conscience is the voice of God within every man that he consistently fails to listen to. Therefore, not only does man break God's laws, but he cannot even live up to the moral law within him. The conscience of man tells him, through the existence of creation, that God exists and that He is all powerful.

> Because that which may be known of God is manifest in them; For God hath shewed it unto them. For the invisible things of him from the creation of the world are clearly seen, being understood by the things that are made, even his eternal power and Godhead; so that they are without excuse (Romans 1:19-20).

Mankind, in the antediluvian, or pre-flood age soon hardened his conscience against God by making that age a sensual playground. Even though they had the godly witness of Enoch and Noah, their preoccupation with sensual pursuits caused them to neglect the warnings of judgment. The result was the destruction of the entire human race except for Noah and his family.

> Noah found grace in the eyes of the LORD (Genesis 6:8).

> And every living substance was destroyed which was upon the face of the ground, both man, and cattle, and the creeping things, and the fowl of the heaven; and they were destroyed from the earth: and Noah only remained alive, and they were with him in the ark (Genesis 7:23).

The Age of Human Government

Because violence was prevalent before the Flood, man was now given the responsibility to carry out capital punishment for murder because of the nobility of human life.

> Whoso sheddeth man's blood, by man shall his blood be shed; for the image of God made he man (Genesis 9:6).

The power of human government over life and death was established to maintain order, and that power is still maintained today through our police and armed forces.

> For he is the minister of God to thee for good. But if thou do that which is evil, be afraid; for he beareth not the sword in vain: for he is the minister of God, a revenger to execute wrath upon him that doeth evil (Romans 13:4).

Humankind, in that day, refused to scatter and fill the whole earth but sought to unify in one location and build the monument of the Tower of Babel to honor themselves, rather than God. After the church age, during the Tribulation, man under the Antichrist will again seek to establish a one-world government to exalt himself. This ungodly unity would be an unrestrained source for the evil imagination of men who would have no regard for the witness of God in their civilization.

> And they said, Go to, let us build a city and a tower, whose top may reach unto heaven; and let us make us a name, lest we be scattered abroad upon the face of the whole earth. And the LORD came down to see the city and the tower, which the children of men builded. And the LORD said, behold the people is one, and they have all one language; and this they begin to do: and nothing shall be restrained from them, which they have imagined to do. Go to, let us go down, and there confound their language, that they may not understand one another's speech. So the LORD scattered them abroad from thence upon the face of the earth; and they left off to build the city (Genesis 11:4-8).

Man, because of his pride and disobedience, again failed to obey God after the judgment of the Flood.

The Age of Promise

The age of promise was initiated by the promise of God which is based upon the grace of God. In that sense, it will never fail or end. It is used in this writing to signify a change in the way that God would now deal with man. God would choose a single individual, Abraham, who would be the progenitor of the Jewish nation and fulfill His promises through him exclusively, rather than through the Gentile nations, as He did previously. The beginning of the age of promise finds God revealing Himself to the patriarchs, the fathers of the Jewish nation such as Abraham, Isaac, and Jacob as they set out for the land of promise. The ages that follow the age of promise do not nullify this age but simply fulfill the promises of God. The age of the law was temporary and would emphasize the righteous requirements of God for mankind. The church age to follow would emphasize the grace of God to meet mans failure to keep the law of God by instituting the promise of the new covenant. The promises of God would all be ultimately fulfilled through Christ, who was the seed of Abraham.

> Now to Abraham and his seed were the promises made. He saith not, and to seeds, as of many; but as of one, And to thy seed, which is Christ (Galatians 3:16).[2]

> Now the LORD had said unto Abram, Get thee out of thy country, and from thy kindred, and from thy fathers house, unto a land that I will show thee: And I will make of thee a great nation, and I will bless thee, and make thy name great; and thou shalt be a blessing; And I will bless thee them that bless thee, and curse him that curseth thee: and in thee shall all families of the earth would be blessed (Genesis 12:1-3).

The blessing upon Abraham was three-fold. First, he was promised personal blessing. This was fulfilled as Abraham became a rich man. Second, he was promised a land and a great nation. This will be ultimately fulfilled through Israel in the Millennial Age, and third, all the families of the earth would be blessed through Abraham. This is largely happening today in the church age when many Gentiles are being saved through the means of the faith of Abraham and becoming a part of the family of God. However, Gentiles have always been a focus of the salvation of God, and many will be saved in the Tribulation and the Millennium.

The Age of the Law

The old covenant containing the law was the preparatory age for the grace of God through Christ. The law was a teacher through every ones failure and inability to keep it.

> Wherefore the law was our schoolmaster to bring us unto Christ, that we might be justified by faith (Galatians 3:24).

The Scriptures are clear that the age of the law did not supersede or replace the age of promise.

> And this I say, that the covenant, that was confirmed before by God in Christ, the law, which was four hundred and thirty years after, cannot disannul, that it should make the promise none effect. For if the inheritance be of the law, it is no more of promise: but God gave it to Abraham by promise (Galatians 3:17-18).

> And all the people answered together, and said, All that the LORD hath spoken we will do. And Moses returned the words of the people unto the LORD (Exodus 19:8).

The people promised God that they would keep His law. The old covenant was based on the promise of man to keep it and illustrated man's failure (inability) to keep his promise to obey God's commands.

Abraham forever served as an example that men are always saved by faith. The law illustrated that the only means of salvation was faith in Christ because of man's failure to completely obey the Law. If we seek to gain salvation by law keeping, we must keep it perfectly because God is perfect. Scripture does not teach sinless perfection here on earth.

> For as many as are of the works of the law are under the curse; for it is written, curseth is every one that continueth not in all things which are written in the book of the law to do them. But that no man is justified by the law in the sight of God, it is evident: for, The just shall live by faith (Galatians 3:10-11).

The Church Age

Christ and His work on the cross is the fulfillment of the new covenant promises to the church. Anticipating His death on the cross, Christ instituted the new covenant with His disciples at the Last Supper.

> And as they were eating Jesus took bread and blessed it, and brake it, and gave it to the disciples, and said, Take, eat; this is my body. And he took the cup, and gave thanks, and gave it unto them saying, Drink ye all of it; For this is my blood of the new testament, which is shed for many for the remission of sins (Matthew 26:26-28).

Two great promises from God are contained in the new covenant. Neither of these promises can be fulfilled through our own efforts.

The first promise is the forgiveness of God for sins:

And I will be merciful to their unrighteousness, and their sins
and their iniquities will I remember no more (Hebrews 8:12).

The second promise is the internal change of a man's
heart which can only be accomplished by God Himself:

. . . I will put my law into their mind, and write them into
their hearts; and I will be to them a God, and they shall
be to me a people (Hebrews 8:10b).

The Millennial Age

God is not finished with Israel as a national entity.
Although the new covenant promises of forgiveness and the
power of inward change by the Holy Spirit are experienced by
the church today, Israel as a nation will experience them in a
greater way in the future. Speaking to the Gentile believers
of Rome, Paul states:

For I would not, brethren, that you should be ignorant of
this mystery, lest ye should be wise in your own conceits,
that blindness in part has happened to Israel, until the
fullness of the Gentiles be come in. And so all Israel shall
be saved: as it is written, there shall come out of Zion the
Deliverer and shall turn away ungodliness from Jacob: For
this is my covenant unto them, when I shall take away their
sins (Romans 11:25-27).

The "fullness of the Gentiles" is a phrase that applies to
the salvation of a large number of Gentiles in the church age.
When the church is removed at the Rapture, God will pour
out His new covenant blessings on the nation of Israel, who

was promised a land in the promises to Abraham. The Bible predicts that Christ will rule over this present earth:

> And the LORD shall be king over all the earth; in that day
> shall there be one LORD, and his name one (Zechariah 14:9).

The paradise that was lost by Adam will be regained by Christ. Anything less than the actual rulership of Christ as King over all the earth would fail to fulfill the promises of God and admit defeat to the forces of evil and rebellion on this present earth.

A new age lasting a thousand years will usher in unparalleled spiritual blessings upon this present earth. Israel and the peoples on the earth will experience these spiritual blessings as never before because Satan will be bound for these one thousand years.

> And he laid hold on the dragon, that old serpent, which is
> the Devil, and Satan, and bound him for a thousand years
> (Revelation 20:2).

The book of Revelation refers to this period of a thousand years six times in chapter 20.[3] Second Peter 3:8 states that time is to the Lord "as a thousand years," indicating a figurative meaning in this passage. There is no reason to interpret the passages in Revelation other than as a literal time period of a thousand years.

The Eternal Age

The mediatorial kingdom of Christ consisting of the one thousand year reign of Christ, upon this present earth will come to an end when Christ Himself delivers up the kingdom to God the Father. All enemies of the kingdom of God will finally be destroyed and then the Eternal State will begin. The last enemy of God and man, that will be destroyed, is death.

> Then cometh the end, when he shall have delivered up the kingdom to God, even the Father; when he shall have put down all rule and all authority and power. For he must reign, till he hath put all enemies under his feet. The last enemy that shall be destroyed is death. For he hath put all things under his feet. But when he saith all things are put under him, it is manifest that he is excepted, which did put all things under him. And when all things are subdued unto him, then shall the Son also himself be subject unto him that put all things under him, that God may be all and all (1 Corinthians 15:24-28).

—14—

The Implications Of
The Grace Of God

While the world glosses over sin by simply calling it "mistakes," the Bible is clear that we are sinners by nature and by choice. When sin in the singular is used in Romans 7-8, it refers to the nature of sin:

> For we know that the law is spiritual: but I am carnal, sold under sin (Romans 7:14).

> We have all broken God's laws in one way or another.

> Whosoever committeth sin transgresseth also the law; For sin is the transgression of the law (I John 3:4).

Nothing less than the grace of God can change this propensity to sin. We have been given a new nature through the Holy Spirit at the new birth.

> Jesus answered, Verily, verily, I say unto thee, Except a man be born of water and of the Spirit, he cannot enter into the kingdom of God. That which is born of the flesh is flesh; and that which is born of the Spirit is spirit (John 3:5-6).

That as sin hath reigned unto death, even so might grace reign through righteousness unto eternal life by Jesus Christ our Lord (Romans 5:21).

For the law of the Spirit of life in Christ Jesus hath made me free from the law of sin and death (Romans 8:2).

First of all, the grace of God teaches the believer about change that results in godly behavior. A life affected by the grace of God will demonstrate this godly change:

For the grace of God that bringeth salvation has appeared to all men, Teaching us that denying ungodliness and worldly lusts, we should live soberly, righteously, and godly, in this present world [age] (Titus 2:11-12).

Secondly, the *doctrine of grace* means that the believer is "separated" or "set apart" unto his God, being purchased by the redemption of the blood of Christ. In light of the sin of fornication, Paul states:

What? Know ye not that your body is the temple of the Holy Ghost [Spirit] which is in you, which ye have of God, and ye are not your own? For ye are bought with a price: therefore, glorify God in your body and in your spirit, which are God's (1 Corinthians 6:19-20).

Thirdly, the blessing of the experiential loving fatherhood of God is promised to the believer who takes personal responsibility to separate himself from the sins of the flesh and spirit as 2 Corinthians 6:14-18; 7:1 declares:

Be ye not unequally yoked together with unbelievers: for what fellowship hath righteousness with unrighteousness?

and what communion hath light with darkness? And what concord hath Christ with Belial? or what part hath he that believeth with an infidel? And what agreement hath the temple of God with idols? For ye are the temple of the living God; as God hath said, I will dwell in them, and walk in them; and I will be their God, and they shall be my people. Wherefore, come out from among them, and be ye separate, saith the Lord, and touch not the unclean thing; And I will receive you, And will be a father unto you, and ye shall be my sons and daughters, saith the Lord Almighty . . . Having therefore these promises, dearly beloved, let us cleanse ourselves from all filthiness of the flesh and spirit, perfecting holiness in the fear of God.

Two Errors in the Early Church being Repeated Today

There were two main errors in the early church concerning the grace of God. These errors are perpetuated in the church today. These errors were both basic abuses of the Bible doctrine of the grace (unmerited favor) of God to man.

The first error regarding grace was legalism. This is the religious persuasion that by keeping certain rules a man can obtain favor from God.[1] In other words, this involves an effort to gain favor from God through works or doing certain things either for initial salvation or to make one-self spiritual. This is an error moving one from faith-orientated living to a performance—mentality.

The second error regarding grace was making it an excuse (license) to sin. The apostle Paul anticipated this argument.

What shall we say then? Shall we continue in sin that grace may abound (Romans 6:1).

The Bible states that the Christian life is always a walk of faith connected to a love for God, which is based on a dependence on the Holy Spirit living within.

> If we live in the Spirit, let us also walk in the Spirit (Galatians 5:25).

> For in Jesus Christ neither circumcision availeth any thing, nor uncircumcision; but faith which worketh by love (Galatians 5:6).

Living by love and faith delivers the believer from either license, or legalism. It seems that the problem of the modern church of the twenty-first century, because of the hedonistic culture in which we live, leans more to license (twisting the doctrine of grace to make it permission to sin) than it does legalism. The believer's co-crucifixion with Christ and his separation from his past life of sin makes the practice of sin a logical incongruity. The apostle Paul in Romans 6:1-2, 6 answers the argument that grace involves a leniency to sin in this manner:

> What shall we say then? Shall we continue in sin that grace may abound? God forbid. How shall we who are dead to sin live any longer in it? . . . Knowing this, that our old man is crucified with him, that the body of sin might be destroyed, that henceforth we should not serve sin.

Concerning Lawful Things not Expressly Forbidden

The believer is given principles in Scripture to cover all behaviour. These principles will protect him from the abuse of Christian liberty as he is being motivated by the love for the Lord in his actions. The first principle is based on concern on how his behaviour will affect his testimony to the weaker brother.[2] Love for the fellow believer and desire for our spiritual growth and that of others should always be the main concerns of the believer. The second principle is how will this behaviour, although not expressly forbidden in the Bible, affect my spiritual life and growth? Does the thing that I am participating in control my life by pushing out spiritual pursuits that are more important?[3] There are some things, while not being sin in themselves, are weights that distract from one's service to the Lord.

> . . . Let us lay aside every weight and the sin which doth so easily beset us, and let us run with patience the race that is set before us (Hebrews 12:1b).

For purpose of example and to be better equipped for ministry, unhindered by distractions, Paul chose to refuse even good things like marriage, the right to financial support, and other perfectly permissible things in order to spread the gospel.

Sin and Moral Insensitivity

As the world progresses more into hedonism and immorality and as these things enter into the homes of the believer through the television, music, and the computer there will be the tendency of the believer to become dull and insensitive to sin itself. The result of this insensitivity will be a chill in the love of the believer for the Lord and others.

> And because iniquity shall abound, the love of many shall wax cold (Matthew 24:12).

The example of the believers in the days of Ezra and Nehemiah is instructive for the modern church as they repented of their disobedience and sin and *trembled* at the hearing of the Word of God. *Trembling* is a word which signifies a "fear" or "reverence" for God that result in an effort to cooperate with God as He works in the believer to accomplish His will.

> Wherefore, my beloved, as you have always obeyed, not as in my presence only, but now much more in my absence, work out your own salvation with fear and trembling. For it is God who worketh in you both to will and to do of his good pleasure (Philippians 2:12-13).

The Pathway to Spiritual Living

Therefore, the path to spiritual living is to first "put off" as a garment, through repentance and confession of sin, the carnal nature and its deeds and to "put on" as a garment the new nature. This is accomplished through the power of the Spirit by the Scriptures.[4] Spiritual change into Christlikeness is accomplished by the Spirit as contemplation through meditation in the Scriptures on the glory of God and Christ, is practiced by the believer.[5] Spiritual energy, or the power of revival occurs when a new realization of the greatness and uniqueness of God and Christ occurs. This is evidenced in the spiritual revival led by Ezra and Nehemiah as well as those in American history. A rediscovery of a genuine worship of God will bring a new zeal in everything that is accomplished for the Lord, including evangelism.

How To Be Filled With The Spirit In This Church Age

> And be not drunk with wine, where in is excess;
> but be filled with the spirit (Ephesians 5:18).

Believers in Christ now live in the age of the Spirit. The Spirit is the true dynamic source of power for a believer who pleases God. Without the filling of the Spirit which is secured by remaining in fellowship with Christ, the believer cannot accomplish anything in a spiritual sense.

> I am the vine, ye are the branches: He that abideth in me, and I in him, the same bringeth forth much fruit: for without me ye can do nothing (John 15:5).

Although every believer is indwelt by the Spirit, he is not necessarily filled with the Spirit. The Bible commands us to be filled with the Spirit. The fact that it is a command means that some believers may not be filled with the Spirit. The Spirit-filled life is a life controlled by God rather than self.

Realize our Complete Spiritual Bankruptcy

A believer needs to come to the realization of the complete bankruptcy and insufficiency of the *self*, which the apostle Paul calls the "flesh," to live a fruitful Christian life. The flesh does not have the ability to live the Christian life because, as far as God is concerned, it possesses no spiritual goodness or spiritual ability.

> For I know that in me (that is, in my flesh,) dwelleth no good thing: for to will is present with me; but how to perform that which is good I find not (Romans 7:18).

Even more distressing, the flesh stands in opposition to God and wars against spiritual things as we see in Romans 8:7:

> Because the carnal mind is enmity against God: for it is not subject to the law of God, neither indeed can be.

In the Christian life the *self* or "flesh" is constantly at war with the Spirit.

> For the flesh lusteth against the Spirit, and the Spirit against the flesh: and these are contrary the one to the other: so that ye cannot do the things that ye would (Galatians 5:17).

No wonder the apostle Paul stated that he had "no confidence in the flesh."[1] A "no confidence" vote to self, the flesh, must always be given. The believer must constantly remain vigilant against the flesh and its propensity to rebel against God. Many believers are defeated at this point. The flesh, or self is powerless to live a life pleasing to God and is actually hostile to God and His purpose for one's life.

Therefore, the source of power must come from the Holy Spirit through the new nature. The new nature is imparted by the Spirit using the Scriptures. It is described in 2 Peter 1:4:

> Whereby are given unto us exceeding great and precious promises: that by these ye might be partakers of the divine nature, having escaped the corruption that is in the world through lust.

Realize the Spirit-Filled Life Glorifies Christ

The Spirit-filled life glorifies Christ. Therefore, if the believer is to be controlled by or filled with the Spirit; he must also have the desire to exalt and glorify Christ rather than himself. The Holy Spirit did not come to exalt and glorify Himself, He came to exalt and glorify Christ.

> He shall glorify me: for he shall receive of mine, and shall show it unto you (John 16:14).

Realize the Spirit-Filled Life is Imparted through the Scriptures

The Spirit-filled life is imparted through the Scriptures. Therefore it is a life of faith, or trust in the Scriptures rather than trust in our intellectual ability to understand events and circumstances or the feelings of the moment in times of difficulties. Christ is glorified and the believer is filled with the Spirit through reverence and obedience to the written Scriptures. The Spirit-filled life is also the Scripture-filled life as seen in Colossians 3:16-17:

Let the word of Christ dwell in you richly in all wisdom; teaching and admonishing one another in psalms and hymns and spiritual songs, singing with grace in your hearts to the Lord. And whatsoever ye do in word or deed, do all in the name of the Lord Jesus, giving thanks to God and the Father by Him.

The fact that the requirements and results of the Spirit-filled life and the life filled with the Scriptures, are the same as seen in Ephesians 5:18-21:

And be not drunk with wine, wherein is excess; but be filled with the Spirit; Speaking to yourselves in psalms and hymns and spiritual songs, singing and making melody in your heart to the Lord; Giving thanks always for all things unto God and the Father in the name of our Lord Jesus Christ; Submitting yourselves one to another in the fear of God.

Realize the Spirit-Filled Life is Accompanied by Praise and Thanksgiving

The Spirit-filled life is accompanied by a heart of praise and thanksgiving. This heart of praise and thanksgiving is united with the fear of God and a submission to Him as recorded in Ephesians 5:19:

Speaking to yourselves in psalms and hymns and spiritual songs, singing and making melody in your heart to the Lord.

Realize the Spirit-Filled Life is the Submitted Life

One must follow the example of Christ in the area of willing submission to God. He was the supreme example of living for the glory of the Father.

> He that speaketh of himself seeketh his own glory: but he that seeketh his glory that sent him, the same is true, and no unrighteous is in him (John 7:18).

The overwhelming requirement and goal for the Spirit-filled life is to live for the glory and praise of Christ.

> And whatsoever ye do in word or deed, do all in the name of the Lord Jesus, giving thanks to God and the Father by him (Colossians 3:17).

The Spirit-filled life consists of much more than just knowing what the Scriptures say. It entails being obedient and submissive to God's commands.

Realize the Spirit-Filled Life will Reflect the Character of Christ

The central aspect of the character of Christ is love. All other characteristics of the fruit of the Spirit, such as joy and peace, define love.

> Envyings, murders, drunkenness, revellings, and such like: of the which I tell you before, as I have also told you in time past, that they which do such things shall not inherit the kingdom of God. But the fruit of the Spirit is

love, joy, peace, longsuffering, gentleness, goodness, faith (Galatians 5:21-22).

Realize the Spirit-Filled Life Recognizes the Excellence of Christ

In addition to a life of submission, the Spirit-filled life must recognize the excellence of Christ. In order to live for the glory of Christ we must reflect, or meditate on His excellence and glory as revealed in 2 Corinthians 3:18 NKJV:

> But we all, with unveiled face, beholding as in a mirror the glory of the Lord, are being transformed [changed] into the same image from glory to glory, just as by the Spirit of the Lord.

Realize the Spirit-Filled Life is a Work in Progress

The filling of the Spirit is a work in progress. The believer is in need of the filling of the Spirit in his life until the Rapture. The filling of the Sprit is a work in progress. Growth and change are part and parcel of the Christian life. It is obvious that God changes the believer as he reflects on the glory of Christ as seen in the mirror of the Scriptures. It is also obvious that this is a process of spiritual growth as it is "from glory to glory." "Walking in the Spirit" is the continuing experience of being "filled with the Spirit." It is a command, and the Greek present tense indicates continuing action.

This I say then, walk in the Spirit, and ye shall not fulfill the lust of the flesh (Galatians 5:16).

A key to "walking in the Spirit" is to be vigilant against sinful attitudes and acts of sin that occur in daily life. As spiritual growth takes place, a sensitivity to sin will follow. This will include a realization of a propensity to grow spiritually cold when sin is tolerated.

Realize the Spirit-Filled Life is a Vigilant Life

The Spirit-filled life takes vigilance against sinful attitudes and acts. The Bible does not teach a "sinless perfection" that can occur in our spiritual lives on this side of eternity. Whenever the light of the Scriptures exposes sin, it must be promptly confessed.

But if we walk in the light, as he is in the light, we have fellowship one with another, and the blood of Jesus Christ, his Son, cleanseth us from all sin. . . . If we confess our sins, he is faithful and just to forgive us our sins, and cleanse us from all unrighteousness (I John 1:7, 9).

This confession will include repentance, or a turning from the sin:

As many as I love, I rebuke and chasten: be zealous, therefore, and repent (Revelation 3:19).

Realize the Spirit-Filled
Life is a Hopeful Life

Overall, the spirit-filled is a life that has hope despite distressing circumstances in the here and now.

Now the God of hope fill you with all joy and peace in believing, that you may abound in hope, through the power of the Holy Ghost (Romans 15:13).

Epilogue

Our Future Hope is in The Person of Jesus, The Christ

- **It is a hope that begins now**

It is a hope that begins now through repentance and faith in Christ but extends beyond this life into the after-life at the resurrection of the just. In fact, the apostle Paul states:

> If in this life only we have hope in Christ, we are of all men most miserable. But now is Christ risen from the dead, and become the firstfruits of them that slept (1 Corinthians 15:19-20).

This hope is not just positive or wishful thinking. It is based on the reality of the resurrection of Christ as a historical event; because He was raised, we will be raised also.

- **It is a hope that comforts because of the veracity of the Scriptures**

For whatsoever things were written aforetime were written for our learning, that we through the patience and comfort of the Scriptures might have hope (Romans 15:4).

- **It is a hope that will not leave us in shame, disappointment or disillusionment**

And hope maketh not ashamed; because of the love of God is shed abroad in our hearts by the Holy Ghost which is given unto us (Romans 5:5).

- **It is a hope that brings rest and peace to the believer**

All are invited to the *rest* of discipleship.

Come unto me, all ye that labour and are heavy laden, and I will give you rest, Take my yoke upon you, and learn of me; for I am meek and lowly in heart: and you shall find rest unto your souls. For my yoke is easy, and my burden is light (Matthew 11:28-30).

There is a final ultimate rest for the believer but it is clear that we enter into it now by faith.

Let us, therefore fear, lest, a promise being left us of entering into his rest, any of you should seem to come short of it. For unto us was the gospel preached, as well as unto them; but the word preached did not profit them, not being mixed with faith in them that heard it. For we which have believed do enter into rest, as he said, As I have sworn in my wrath, if they shall enter into my rest:

although the works were finished from the foundation of the world (Hebrews 4:1-3).

- **It is a hope that is futuristic**

Hope is an essential part of salvation looking forward into a future with Christ in the Millennium and the Eternal State. We are saved to the realm of hope.

> For we are saved by hope: but hope that is seen is not hope: for what a man seeth, why doth he yet hope for? (Romans 8:24).

In other words, for the believer, the best is yet ahead. We enter into this hope now through trust in Christ for our eternal salvation and deliverance from spiritual defeat.

The believers of Old Testament times have not entered the final rest, even though they, led by Joshua, entered the Promised Land. For if Joshua had given them rest, God would not have spoken later about another day: There remains then a Sabbath rest for the people of God.[1] This future rest, for the people of God, is the glorious Millennium where there will be peace among men and a full knowledge of God upon the earth.[2]

- **It is a hope that cannot fail because Jesus is the Messiah**

The hope that brings a rest of peace for America in crisis is an individual hope in Christ rather than hope in a human leader or in government itself. Any human leader will fail us, but there is no disappointment in Jesus Christ because He is all that He promised to be. His resurrection is proof that His death atoned for us and that He is the promised Messiah:

> And declared to be the Son of God with power, according to the spirit of holiness, by the resurrection from the dead (Romans 1:4).

In this age,
Christ can set everything right
in the individual believing heart;

In the age to come,
He will set all things right.

Afterword

Since the main body of this book has been written there have been news events of apparent big government overreach. One example has been the IRS targeting of conservative political groups for special scrutiny. The second example is the collection of data consisting of phone records and e-mails of millions of Americans for security purposes. In addition to this, it is come to light that the government is building a huge data center for security in Bluffdale, Utah, capable of collecting three billion phone records in a day.[1] When national security director Keith Alexander was asked by congress, "Does the technology exist to give the ability to listen to American's telephone calls and read their e-mails?" he replied, "The government does not have the authority to do so." Judge Andrew Napolitano, a Fox News contributor felt Alexander lied by changing the word *ability* to *authority* in his answer.[2] On the same newscast it was reported that FBI director Robert Moeller admitted that drones have been used on American soil. Some people such as Senator Rand Paul of Kentucky and Judge Napolitano believe the keeping of the phone records and e-mails of ordinary Americans is a violation of the "no search without probable cause" provision in the Fourth Amendment. [3]

At the end of the age people will give up their privacy and freedom for the promised of security from the state.

> While people are saying, 'Peace and safety,' destruction will come on them suddenly, as labor pains on a pregnant woman, and they will not escape (1 Thessalonians 5:3 NIV).

Prophetic scholar John Walvood, in his commentary, writes regarding 1 Thessalonians 5:3: [4]

> Apparently the world situation at the beginning of the Day of the Lord will provide a false basis for peace. This may be accomplished by a strengthened "United Nations" or world organization.

First Thessalonians 5:3 does not say people are asking for peace and safety. Apparently they think peace and safety had arrived. This corresponds exactly with the two halves of the Tribulation. The first half will be characterized by a settlement of the Israel-Arab-Palestinian crises and an apparent world unity under the Antichrist. The second half will be characterized by persecution of the Jews by the Antichrist, conflict among nations as they approach Jerusalem and the destruction of the Antichrist and his armies when Christ returns. When Christ returns, He will begin to set everything right in His Kingdom.

Suggested Reading

Andrews, Samuel. *Christianity and Anti-Christianity in Their Final Conflict* (1898; reprint, Greenville, S.C.: Bob Jones University Press, 1991).

Beale, David O. *In Pursuit of Purity: American Fundamentalism Since 1850.* Greenville, S.C.: Bob Jones University Press, 1986.

_____. *The Mayflower Pilgrims.* Greenville, S.C.: Bob Jones University Press, 2000.

Bietzel, Barry. *Biblica: The Bible Atlas.* Hauppauge, N.Y.: Global Book Publishing, 2006.

Black, Jim Nelson. *When Nations Die: America on the Brink, Ten Warning Signs of a Culture in Crisis.* Wheaton: Tyndale House Publishers, 1994.

Bobgan, Martin, and Deidre Bobgan. *Psycho Heresy.* Santa Barbara, CA.: EastGate Publishers, 1987.

Cromer, Ronald J. *Abnormal Psychology 2nd ed.* New York: W. H. Freeman & Co., 1995.

Cumby, Constance. *The Hidden Dangers of the Rainbow: The New Age Movement and the Coming Age of Barbarism.* Portland: Video Bible Library, 1983.

Fisher, David. World *History for Christian Schools.* Greenville, S.C.: Bob Jones University Press, Textbook Division, 1984.

Froese, Arno. *How Democracy will Elect the Antichrist.* West Columbia, S.C.: Olive Press, 1997.

Geller, Pamela, and Robert Spencer. *The Post-American Presidency, The Obama Administration's War on America.* N.Y.: Threshold Editions, a division of Simon & Schuster, Inc., 2010.

Guinness, Os, and John Seel, eds. *No God But God.* Chicago: Moody Press, 1992.

Hart, Benjamin. *Faith and Freedom: The Christian Roots of American Liberty.* Addison, Tex.: Lewis and Stanley, 1990.

Hitchcock, Mark. *Iran: The Coming Crisis, Radical Islam, Oil and the Nuclear Threat.* Sisters, OR: Multnomah Publishers, Inc., 2006.

Jasper, William, F., *Global Tyranny . . . Step by Step. The United Nations and the Emerging New World Order.* Appleton, WI.: Western Islands Publishers, 1992.

Marrs, Texe. *Dark Secrets of the New Age.* Wheaton: Crossway Books, 1987.

McCallum, Dennis. *The Death of Truth.* Minneapolis: Bethany House Publishers, 1996.

Miller, Elliot. *A Crash Course on the New Age Movement.* Grand Rapids: Baker Book House, 1993.

Morris, Dick and Eileen McGann. *Here Come the Black Helicopters! UN Global Governance and the Loss of Freedom.* New York: Broadside Books, an imprint of Harper Collins Publishers, 2012.

Pentecost, Dwight. *Things to Come: A Study in Biblical Eschatology.* Grand Rapids: Zondervan Publishing House, 1969.

Ryrie, Charles Caldwell. *Ryrie Study Bible* KJV. Chicago: Moody Press, 1994.

Stormer, John A. *The Death of a Nation.* Florissant, MO.: Liberty Bell Press, 1968.

Szasz, Thomas. *The Myth of Psychotherapy.* Garden City, N.Y.: Doubleday Anchor Press, 1978.

Walvoord, John F. *Armageddon, Oil and the Middle East Crisis.* Grand Rapids: Zondervan Publishing House, 3rd printing, 1990.

_____. *The Thessalonian Epistles.* Grand Rapids: Zondervan Publishing House, 9th printing, 1974.

Notes

Preface

1. King James Version cited unless otherwise noted.
2. The Bible defines eternal life as "the ages unto the ages" (*aionion*). The word of God indicates that history is divided into dispensations which are also called ages.

Ages To Come Chart

1. Acts 2.
2. Thessalonians 5:3-4.
3. Daniel 9:27.

Introduction

1. Fox News. "Hannity," Sean Hannity, host, Feb. 20, 2012. Discussion of the Santorum's Republican Campaign in Ohio.
2. Texe Marrs, *Dark Secrets of the New Age*. Elliot Miller, *A Crash Course on the New Age Movement*. Constance Cumby, *The Hidden Dangers of the Rainbow*.
3. Ibid., Miller, 54.
4. Dick Morris and Eileen McGann, *Here Come the Black Helicopters*, 15.

5. William F. Jasper, *Global Tyranny…Step by Step, iv.*
6. Pamela Geller with Robert Spencer, *The Post-American Presidency, The Obama Administration's War on America*, 26. This book is excellent for further details in Chapter One, "Obama and American Exceptionalism," on how International laws can and will affect America's freedom.

Chapter 1: *What is the World Has Gone Wrong*

1. According to Romans 11 Israel remains God's chosen nation, set aside in this present age. A remnant is being brought into the body of Christ, which is the Church.
2. Romans 9:14-24.
3. The Bible speaks of a day in the future when national Israel will be saved by the Messiah and restored to a place of blessing to the world. "And so all Israel shall be saved: as it is written, There shall come out of Zion the Deliverer, and shall turn away ungodliness from Jacob" (Romans 11:26).
4. The baptism of the Spirit into Christ and His body, the universal church, is the unifying factor bringing all people, together from different ethnic groups and social classes. "For by one Spirit are we all baptized into one body, whether we be Jews or Gentiles, whether we be bond or free; and have made all to drink into one Spirit" (1 Corinthians 12:13). The church age began at the Jewish Day of Pentecost as recorded in Acts 2 and is completed (concludes) with the removal of believers from earth to Heaven, at the Rapture.
5. The Holy Spirit of God and man himself both cooperate with God in election. The election of God is not capricious and does not preclude the choice of man. "…God hath from the beginning chosen you to salvation through sanctification of the Spirit and belief of the truth" (2 Thessalonians 2:13b).

6. 1 Timothy 2:1-4. "I exhort therefore, that, first of all, supplications, prayers, intercessions, and giving of thanks, be made for all men; For kings, and for all that are in authority; that we may lead a quiet and peaceable life in all godliness and honesty. For this is good and acceptable in the sight of God our Saviour; Who will have all men to be saved, and to come unto the knowledge of the truth."

7. Fox News, "Happening Now" with Jenna Lee and Jon Scott, January 23, 2012.

8. Fox News, "Happening Now," Jenna Lee's interview with Gordon Chang, October 9, 2012.

9. All panelists on Anchor Bret Bair's 6 o'clock EST News Special Report believed there was a good chance of an Israeli invasion of Iran that would dramatically change the world situation as we know it now. Fox News. Feb. 6, 2012.

10. Hope in Hebrew is *batah*. The Septuagint, the ancient Greek translation of the Old Testament, translates this word with *elpizo*, meaning "to hope" as used in the New Testament. The idea of a hope, which provides security, is only in God.

11. The believer will "…rejoice in the hope of the glory of God" (Romans 5:2b). "And hope maketh not ashamed [does not disappoint]; because the love of God is shed abroad in our hearts by the Holy Spirit which is given to us" (5:5).

Chapter 2: *I have Seen the Enemy—It is "I"*

1. http://nation.foxnews.com/paul-harvey/2012/03/21/1965-if-i-were-devil-warning-nation-paul-harvey; accessed November 12, 2012.

2. Romans 1:28. The whole chapter needs to be read to understand the downward slide of mankind when they reject the truth.

3. John 14:6. "Jesus saith unto him, I am the way, the truth, and the life: no man cometh unto the Father, but by me." For further discussion on agnostic pluralism and political correctness *Faith and Freedom* by Benjamin Hart is recommended reading.
4. For further discussion on post-modernism see recommended reading Dennis McCallum's book, *The Death of Truth.*
5. Ronald J. Cromer, *Abnormal Psychology*, 2nd ed., 4.
6. Fox News, "Happening Now," with Jenna Lee and John Scott. Dec. 15, 2012.
7. *No God But God*, ed. by Os Guiness and John Seel is recommended reading on the influence of psychology as superceding religion today. See especially the essay by Guinesss, "America's Last Men and Their Magnificent Talking Cure." 132.
8. For more about the religious backgrounds of these men read *The Myth of Psychotherapy* by Thomas Szasz and *Psychoheresy* by Martin and Deidre Bobgan.

Chapter 3:   *History Does - Repeat Itself*

1. Genesis 6:1, 2.
2. A progressive is one who favors reform, improvement, and progress through government action. Teddy Roosevelt was the first president to carry out the reforms of the progressives wanting a "square deal" for everyone. Franklin Delanor Roosevelt with his entitlement programs after World War II and Lyndon Johnson's "Great Society" continued to extend the central government's role in American society.
3. Revelation speaks of a man who will rise to head a Ten-Kingdom Empire at the end of the age. The empire will be centered in a seven hilled city which many conservative

commentators identify with Rome. The mystery of Babylon has both a central religious and economic element (Revelation 13:1-18; 17-18).

4. John A. Stormer, *The Death of a Nation*, 154-155.

5. UPI—*Daily Bulletin*, Anderson, Ind., September 20, 1967.

6. Revelation 13:17. "And that no man might buy or sell, save [except] he that had the mark, or the name of the beast, or the number of his name."

Chapter 4:   *The Lessons of History in Religious Past*

1. *The Mayflower Pilgrims* by David Beale is recommended reading for a look at the character and the preaching of the pilgrims.

2. Jonathan Edwards, sermon "Sinners in the Hand of an Angry God" preached on July 8, 1741 in Enfield, CT.

3. "A Faithful Narrative of a Surprising Work of God" is Edward's own account of the conversion of many hundreds of souls in North Hampton and other nearby communities. http://www.jonathan-edwards.org/Narrative.html; accessed May 8, 2012.

4. For a concise reading on the existence of Fundamentalism since 1850, *In Pursuit of Purity* by David Beale is recommended.

5. Ibid. 36, 37.

6. Jim Nelson Black, *When Nations Die, America on the Brink: Ten Warning Signs of a Culture in Crisis*, 17.

7. http://www.lorencollins.net/tytler.html; accessed May 10, 2012.

8. Ephesians 5:14-6:3. Husband-wife and parent-child relationships are discussed in this section.

9. 2 Timothy 3:2a-3b.

10. *US News and World Report*, "Broken Bond: When A Child Hates A Parent," December 2009, 77.

11. Ibid.

12. Ephesians 5:18-6:4.

Chapter 5:   *The Characteristics of the Spiritual Revival Led By Ezra and Nehemiah*

1. Ezra 6:19; Nehemiah 13.
2. Nehemiah 9:32.
3. Nehemiah 9:7-31.
4. Deuteronomy 6:4-6. "Hear, O Israel: The LORD our God is one LORD: And thou shalt love the LORD thy God with all thine heart, and with all thy soul, and with all thy might. And these words, which I command thee this day, shall be in thine heart."
5. Black, *When Nations Die*, 8.

Chapter 6:   *Rebellion in the Mystery Form of the Kingdom*

1. Revelation 11:18b "...and shouldest destroy them which destroy the Earth."
2. Regarding Daniel 4:25, "The king's illness was boanthropy (imaging himself to be an animal and acting accordingly). A condition that has been observed in modern times." Charles Caldwell Ryrie, *Ryrie Study Bible*, 1275.
3. Recommended Bible reading on the mystery form of the kingdom and the judgment of the nations is Matthew 13; 25:1-13; 31-46.
4. James, a leader of the Jerusalem council agreed with the assessment of Peter when he said, "Simeon hath declared how God at the first did visit the Gentiles [nations], to take out of them a people for his name" (Acts 15:14). After this is accomplished, God would restore the kingdom to Israel (Acts 15:15-17).
5. 2 Peter 3:9. "The Lord is not slack concerning his promise, as some men count slackness; but is longsuffering us-ward,

not willing that any should perish, but that all should come to repentance."

6. Key passages on the downfall of Lucifer who became Satan are Isaiah 14:12-18 and Ezekiel 28:11-19.

7. "Thine heart was lifted up because of thy beauty, thou has corrupted thy wisdom by reason of thy brightness: I will cast thee to the ground, I will lay thee before kings, that they may behold thee" (Ezekiel 28:17). His goal of independent autonomy is indicated in the 5 "I Wills." "*I will* ascend into heaven, *I will* exalt my throne above the stars of God, *I will* sit also upon the mount of the congregation, in the sides of the north: *I will* ascend above the heights of the clouds; *I will* be like the most high" (Isaiah 14:13-14). (Emphasis added by author.)

8. Genesis 3:5.

9. Ephesians 2:2. "Wherein in time past ye walked according to the course of this world, according to the prince of the power of the air, the spirit that now worketh in the children of disobedience."

10. The ancient Book of Job gives us insight into Satan's role as the accuser of Job. "Now there was a day when the sons of God came to present themselves before the LORD, and Satan came also among them. And the LORD said unto Satan, from Whence comest thou? Then Satan answered the LORD, and said, From going to and fro in the earth, and from walking up and down in it. And the LORD said unto Satan, Hast thou considered my servant Job, that there is none like him in the earth, a perfect and upright man, one that feareth God, and escheweth [shun] evil? Then Satan answered the LORD, and said, Doth Job fear God for nought? Hast not thou made a hedge around him, and about his house, and about all that he hath on every side? thou hast blessed the work of his hands, and his substance is increased in the land" (1:6-10).

11. These events are all recorded in Revelation 12. These 1260 days in Revelation 12:6 are the last three and a half years of the Tribulation. Although the first three and a half years are much like this present age when a pseudo peace engulfs the world, the last half of the Tribulation will be characterized by intense persecution of Israel and striving among nations.

12. Revelation 11:7 reads: "And when they shall have finished their testimony testimony, the beast that ascendeth out of the bottomless pit shall make war against them, and shall overcome them, and kill them." After the testimony of the two witnesses in the first half of the Tribulation the Beast (Antichrist) will ascend out of the netherworld (in Greek the *abussos* or the "abyss"). This happens after the Antichrist receives his deadly wound and is healed (an imitation of the resurrection of Christ) of Revelation 13:3.

13. Dwight Pentecost points out that the Greek word *polemos* translated battle in Revelation 16:14 signifies a campaign rather than a single battle. *Things to Come, A Study in Biblical Eschatology*, 340.

14. Pentecost points out that Rosh is the translation of "chief prince of Tubal" that refers to the king of the Russian Empire and Magog which is the land north of Israel and north of the Caspian Sea where the Scythian tribes settled north of the Caspian and Black seas. Persia is modern Iran in *Things to Come*, 328-329. Mark Hitchcock, although he differs some on the origins of these ancient names also identifies the first two nations of this northern confederacy as modern Russia and Iran, the present bitter enemy of Israel in *Iran: The Coming Crisis, Radical Islam, Oil and the Nuclear Threat* in Chap. 7 titled "The Iranian-Russian Connection." This book is recommended reading on the trends in the modern day that foreshadow the Great Tribulation.

15. The vision of the dry bones is in Ezekiel 37 and the Balfour declaration by the British promised a national home for the Jewish people. David Fisher, *World History for Christian Schools*, 612.

16. Ezekiel 38:21.

17. Ezekiel 38:22.

18. Ezekiel 38:13.

19. An interesting article in TIME Magazine details "Putin's Pride in Democratic Reform and Russia's Need for Oil" by Fareed Zarakia, "The Putin Paradox: Tyrant or Saviour?" Feb. 20, 2012, 21.

20. Russia is giving arms to Syria and both Russia and China refuse to support UN sanctions as Syria's mercilessly crack down on dissenters in that country. Fox News. America's Newsroom, with Bill Hemmer and Martha McCallum. Jan. 22, 2012; Feb. 6, 2012.

21. Hitchcock places Revelation 16 and the bowl judgments, including the Kings of the East at the end of the Tribulation period. Hitchcock, *Iran: The Coming Crisis*, 204-205.

Chapter 7: *A Revived Roman Empire: Neo-Democracy*

1. The vision of the images of legs and feet are described as: "His legs of iron, his feet part of iron and part of clay" (Daniel 2:33).

2. See the remarkable book written by Samuel Andrews in 1898 *Christianity and Anti-Christianity in Their Final Conflict* where he states that democracy is a natural companion of socialism and observes the trends of the modern age which will lead to the rise of democracy combined with socialism. He also predicts a conflict between Christianity and Islam at the end of the age. For more information on this neo-democracy *How Democracy Will Elect the Antichrist* by Arno Froese is recommended reading.

3. John 8:32. "And ye shall know the truth, and the truth shall make you free."

4. There were other influences upon the founders of our nation such as the emphasis of reason which came from the Enlightenment. Many of the founders combined a philosophy of personal piety with a politically convenient idea that there was a common moral philosophy rooted simply in human reason which could give the foundation for government and a good citizenry. The ideals of democracy go back to the Magna Charta and English tradition. John Locke applied Protestant theology and principles to the ordering of government by arguing that government is a compact between the governments that could be dissolved by the governed.

5. The modern division of the Near East is an outcome of the division of that area between Britain and France after the collapse of the Ottoman Empire in 1917. At this time Palestine became an international entity. Barry Bietzel, *Biblica: The Bible Atlas*, 47.

CHAPTER 8: *The Unexpected Great Event*

1. This exactly corresponds with the teaching concerning the "Day of the Lord" which is preceded by a time when "…they shall say, Peace and safety; then sudden destruction cometh upon them, as travail upon a woman with child; and they shall not escape" (1 Thessalonians 5:3). Chaos occurs when the Antichrist declares he is god. Increasing plagues from God also occur which end with the second coming of Christ at the Day of the Lord to set up His kingdom over the earth.

2. Daniel 11 covers important rulers as they pertain to Israel starting from Darius the Persian to the Antichrist. Daniel 11:21-35 describes the historical person who was Antiochus

and 11:36-45 describes the one whom he typifies, the Antichrist of the end of the age.

3. Revelation 17:12-14 seems to describe action at a conference table and describes the unity of a willing acquiescence to the Antichrist. "And the ten horns which thou sawest are ten kings, which have received no kingdom as yet, but receive power as kings one hour with the beast. These have one mind, and shall give their power and authority to the beast."

Chapter 9: *A Holding Stage to the Next Great Event*

1. In Ephesians 3:4-10 and 1 Corinthians 15:51 Paul states that he was chosen to bear the mystery of the church age and the mystery of the Rapture of the Church. This was not revealed in the Old Testament era but is revealed to us today through the writings of Paul.

2. 1 Corinthians 1:22. "For the Jews require a sign, and the Greeks seek after wisdom."

3. The Rapture is referred to in 1 Corinthians 1:8; 5:5; 15:51-57; 2 Corinthians 1:14; Philippians 1:6-10; 2:16, and 1 Thessalonians 4:13-18.

4. 1 Thessalonians 1:10. "And to wait for his Son from heaven, whom he raised from the dead, even Jesus, which delivered us from the wrath to come."

5. 1 Thessalonians 1:10; 2:19; 3:13; 4:18; 5:23 presents the entrance into heaven of Jesus with believers rather than His arrival to earth with believers.

6. 2 Thessalonians 2:5-6 indicates that Paul had taught prophetic events while he was in Thessalonica, including doctrine about the hinderer.

7. 2 Peter 2:5. "And spared not the old world, but saved Noah the eighth person, a preacher of righteousness, bringing in the flood upon the world of the ungodly."

8. 2 Thessalonians 2:11. "And for this cause God shall send them strong delusion, that they should believe the lie." The lie is of a particular sort, "the lie."

9. "Nevertheless, when the son of man cometh, shall he find faith on the earth?" (Luke 18:8b). Faith here is defined as the faith, i.e. the revealed body of truth about God. The revealed truth in the Scriptures seems to have been largely obliterated among mankind at the coming of Christ. This would seem to refer more to the time of the Rapture than to the Second Coming as many of the Jewish nation come to know Christ during the Tribulation period and the nation is supernaturally protected by God during the last half of the Tribulation period.

Chapter 10: *Will the Real Christ Please Stand Up?*

1. Matthew 24:24a.

2. John 5:33-39.

3. 1 Corinthians 15:5-7. "And that he was seen of Cephas [Peter], then of the twelve: After that, he was seen of about five hundred brethren at once; of whom the greater part remain until this present, but some are fallen asleep. After that, he was seen of James; then, of all the apostles."

4. Acts 26:26b.

5. John contends: "That which was from the beginning, which we have heard, which we have seen with own eyes, which we have looked upon, and our hands have handled, of the Word of life" (I John 1:1). Luke is careful to say "And he [Jesus] took it, [the fish] and did eat before them" (Luke 24:43).

6. Acts 1:3 New American Standard Version.

7. John 20:17, 24-29. Mary clung to Him after she saw Him after His resurrection and the doubting disciple Thomas touched His side and His hands to personally examine the wounds of Christ which He had suffered at the cross.

8. Matthew 27:62-66; 28:11-15.

9. This is testified by Christ Himself: "I am the bread of Life…" (John 6:35a). John further testifies that "…God has given to us eternal life, and this life is in his Son" (I John 5:11b).

10. Passages such as Philippians 2:5-8; John 5:19; 8:28, 54, and Isaiah 41:8 indicate Jesus came as a servant to do the will of the Father.

11. Luke 4:1.

Chapter 11: *The Genuine New Age*

1. Hebrews 1:2a. "Hath in these last days spoken unto us by his Son."

2. The Tribulation period is a seven year period of time predicted in the books of Daniel (9:24-27) and Revelation (11:2-3; 12:6, 14). Jesus refers to the last three and a half years as "Great Tribulation" (Matthew 24:21). According to the Jewish calendar it is divided into two periods of 1260 days or 42 months.

3. Nuclear warfare causes atmospheric changes which would bring an over- flowing rain and pestilence in its wake.

4. Matthew 24:7.

5. Revelation 7.

6. Revelation 20:1-6; Isaiah 1:26; 9:7; 11:2-5.

7. Zechariah 10:10a. "I will bring them again also out of the land of Egypt."

8. Jeremiah 31:33; Revelation 20:1-3; 2 Corinthians 4:4.

9. Jeremiah 30:19-20; Ezekiel 47:22; Zechariah 10:8-9.

Chapter 12: *Final Events for Mankind*

1. Revelation 20:4-22:21; Colossians 1:20.

2. Revelation 20:7-9.

3. Revelation 20:11-15.
4. Revelation 19:20; 20:10.
5. Ephesians 2:2.
6. Hebrews 12:23. "...the general assembly and the church of the first-born..." refers to the church whereas "...the spirits of just men made perfect" refers to Old Testament believers and the Tribulation saints.
7. Matthew 5:5. "Blessed are the meek: for they shall inherit the earth."
8. Charles Ryrie argues that they represent redeemed people who are gloried, crowned and enthroned, *Ryrie Study Bible*.
9. Pentecost, *Things to Come*, p. 209.
10. Revelation 5:10.
11. Luke 19:17-19.
12. Pentecost, 578.
13. Revelation 21:22.
14. Revelation 21:23.
15. Revelation 21:25.
16. Revelation 21:26.

Chapter 13: *The Panorama of the Ages*

1. Philippians 1:21a; 3:10a.
2. In Galatians 3:16 the genealogy of Christ is traced back to Abraham in Matthew who presents Christ as the Messiah/King of the Jews.
3. Revelation 20:2-6.

Chapter 14: *The Implication of the Grace of God*

1. The books of Galatians and Colossians were written to specific churches to deal with this problem. "Touch not,

taste not, handle not" was the motto of the churches who practiced legalism.

2. Passages such as 1 Corinthians 8 and Romans 14-15 deal with this subject.

3. Passages such as Romans 14:22-23 and 1 Corinthians 7:29-31; 9:1-27 deal with these answers.

4. Ephesians 4:22-24.

5. 2 Corinthians 3:18.

Chapter 15: *How to be filled with the Spirit in this Church Age*

1. Philippians 3:3.

Epilogue

1. Hebrews 4:8-9 NIV.

2. Isaiah 11:9-10.

Afterword

1. Fox News, Special Report, 6.00 p. m. Brett Baier, June 10, 2013.

2. Fox News, Studio B, Shepherd Smith, June 19, 2013.

3. Fox News, Your World, Neil Cavuto, June 21, 1913.

4. John Walvoord, *The Thessalonian Epistles*, 18.